# TALES FROM THE
# BYU COUGARS
## SIDELINE

## A COLLECTION OF THE GREATEST COUGAR STORIES EVER TOLD

BY

BRAD ROCK

SPORTS
PUBLISHING

Sports Publishing books may be purchased in bulk at special discounts for sales promotion, corporate gifts, fund-raising, or educational purposes. Special editions can also be created to specifications. For details, contact the Special Sales Department, Sports Publishing, 307 West 36th Street, 11th Floor, New York, NY 10018 or sportspubbooks@skyhorsepublishing.com.

Sports Publishing® is a registered trademark of Skyhorse Publishing, Inc.®, a Delaware corporation.

Visit our website at www.sportspubbooks.com

10 9 8 7 6 5 4 3 2 1

Library of Congress Cataloging-in-Publication Data is available on file.

ISBN: 978-1-61321-339-1

Printed in the United States of America

*To Audrey, Preston, Allison,*

*Meredith, Jordan and Lauren*

———————————————

# Contents

# Introduction

Whenever former athletes, coaches or sports media members gather in an informal setting, the conversation usually involves stories of the great plays and players, unusual characters and funny moments. They share anecdotes of the day one player did this, the time another player said that. Often the characters and events surrounding a game are more interesting than the game itself.

The stories evolve as years pass, but the substance remains. One of the challenges of writing a book like this one is deciding which and whose version of a particular story to use. Occasionally two or more people remember the same event differently. This book attempts to keep all stories as accurate as possible. In instances where memory must serve, the tales are simply as accurate as the memories of those involved.

The bulk of items in this book come from BYU's golden football era, from the late 1970s through the early 1990s. It is neither a chronological compilation nor a comprehensive effort. It is merely a recounting of legendary stories surrounding BYU football—an "oral history" of the players, coaches and plays that made up the program.

*Tales from the BYU Cougars Sideline* is what you might hear if you went to dinner with Chuck Cutler, Danny Plater, Robbie Bosco, Max Hall, Val Hale, or LaVell Edwards.

It's tales from the sidelines, but also the locker rooms, press boxes, airlines and team hotels.

At best, it's a mostly humorous insight into the inner workings of a major college football program. At very least, you can amaze your friends with your knowledge of BYU minutiae.

Brad Rock
March 2013

# Chapter 1

## *LaVell Edwards*

BYU football, for all intents and purposes, was built by LaVell Edwards. He *was* BYU football. Yet as prominent as he became, not everyone knew him.

For a time he was retained by a housing development in the St. George, Utah area to act as a spokesman/representative. The company used Edwards in its ads, and he occasionally made appearances at the model homes to help convince buyers this was *the* place to live.

The developer called Edwards to say a retired couple was about to buy a house, but he wanted to impress them by having Edwards present. The coach said he would be there on the appointed day.

When the couple arrived at the model home, Edwards spoke amiably with them. The developer made it a point to let the couple know he and the coach were friends—nothing like bringing out high-powered people to close a deal.

As the couple walked out, the wife turned to her husband and said, "Think of it! We're going to be living just down the street from Frank Layden!"

* * * * *

Not everyone cared who LaVell was, either.

Long ago, Edwards and a friend named Cy Kimball were in San Francisco, where they hailed a cab. As the car moved toward its destination, the driver began making small talk, asking where they were from.

Kimball told him they were from Utah. "Do you know who

*LaVell Edwards struck a familiar pose on the sidelines for 29 years.*
*(Photo by Mark Philbrick, BYU Photo)*

this guy is?" he said, pointing to Edwards.

"No."

"It's LaVell Edwards."

No response.

"You've never heard of him?"

"Nope."

"He's coach of the BYU football team," said Kimball emphatically.

The cab driver thought for a moment, then in unimpressed cabbie fashion, replied, "Yeah, well, he's not very big in San Francisco."

* * * * *

Occasionally he wasn't even very big in Utah County.

Edwards regularly attended the LDS temple, even during his busy years as a coach. One day he showed up to attend a session at the Timpanogos Temple in Utah County. A woman at the reception desk saw Edwards and said, "You look really familiar."

"Oh?" said Edwards.

"Yes. I think I know you. Did you go to Ogden High School?"

No," said Edwards.

"Did you work at the Depot in Ogden?"

"No."

"How do I know you?" she continued. "I know I know you from somewhere. You're real familiar. What do you do for a living?"

"Well," said Edwards, somewhat embarrassed, "I've coached a football game or two at BYU in my time."

Then she knew. "Oh, my goodness! My niece's husband just got a job with you! I'm so sorry!"

* * * * *

Edwards wasn't one to endure extreme temperatures if he didn't have to. Some years it was a running joke among players to see how quickly he would call off practice if rain, sleet or snow loomed.

Jim McMahon was among the most avid at monitoring how quickly they would finish. On a cold day, he would say in the huddle, "He's gonna call practice in two more plays."

Maybe it would be three plays. Perhaps one. But sure enough, not long after, practice would end.

Which probably explains why he liked playing in the San Diego Holiday Bowl so much.

\* \* \* \* \*

Edwards developed a close relationship with Grant Teaff, the respected coach of the Baylor Bears. Teaff sent Edwards a pair of Dallas Cowboy-colored, gray-and-blue cowboy boots as a gift one year.

Edwards wore his boots into a staff meeting, telling everyone where he got them. He always sat in the same chair, tipping it back so he could rest his feet on the table. But now he had new boots to show off.

In the middle of the discussion, the chair flipped out from under him. Down went the coach.

"All you could see were those new boots sticking up above the table," said Garth Hall, a former BYU assistant coach.

Edwards jumped up, righted the chair, patted his stomach and hitched his pants in the old familiar gestures.

Nobody even laughed.

"Everyone was in so much shock, so surprised, that we decided we better not say anything. But I was busting a gut trying not to laugh," said Hall.

\* \* \* \* \*

BYU's coaching staff was noted through the Edwards years as being cohesive and stable. In fact, much of the Cougars' success has been credited to his ability to keep most of his staff intact.

That, however, doesn't mean it was a Sunday school.

There were egos. There were personality conflicts. There were flat-out bad feelings, at times.

Not to mention times when they didn't accomplish much.

During one coaching staff meeting, Edwards's secretary cracked open the door and told him he had a phone call and that he would likely want to take it in his office.

Time passed after Edwards left the coaches' meeting. Fifteen minutes turned into 30.

Still no LaVell.

Meanwhile, the assistants coaches, who hadn't been getting along, sat in the room for 45 minutes, waiting for his return.

Nobody spoke the entire 45 minutes.

Finally, when they felt they had waited long enough, they left.

Edwards never did return. He forgot about the meeting entirely.

\* \* \* \* \*

It was no secret that Jim McMahon didn't like school. He didn't much care for BYU, either.

But that doesn't mean he got off the hook all the time. Ann Edwards Cannon, LaVell's daughter, remembers the opposite.

One night when she was still in college, she walked over to the coach's office to see her father. In those days, Edwards had a small space in the Smith Fieldhouse.

When she arrived, she noted McMahon in the corner of the office, sitting at a card table with a stack of books beside him.

When she inquired about the star quarterback, Edwards said, "He's not going anywhere until his studies are done."

Even superstar quarterbacks, it seemed, had to answer to the coach.

\* \* \* \* \*

Kids get used to their father being the focus of attention when he's a well-known football coach like Edwards. But that doesn't mean they always like it, even as adults.

Several years ago, Ann and her family were with the LaVell and wife Patti at Christmas time. They had decided to all go to Temple Square in Salt Lake City to enjoy the annual lighting ceremony.

It was designed as a family outing, and Ann and husband Ken's children were expecting to spend the evening with their grandparents.

But shortly after arriving, a couple from out of state recognized Edwards. As the saying goes, that was all she wrote. The couple flanked him on both sides and peppered him with questions, effectively cutting him off from the rest of the family for the entire ceremony.

Oddly enough, the BYU fans didn't seem the least bit aware they were monopolizing Edwards' time.

When you're LaVell Edwards, *everyone* thinks they're family.

* * * * *

There were advantages to being in the Edwards clan, though. He had a lot of friends and contacts.

One of his special talents was getting connected with the right people. That usually meant a deal here, a freebie there. Everyone, it seemed, was happy to comp LaVell. Conversely, Edwards was always generous with others.

"He had a talent for getting hooked up," said Ann. "We always got to go to the drive-ins for free, he always knew the cousin of an uncle, even before he was the head coach. He was always getting a deal at a sporting good store, Sizzler…People would just say 'Go ahead, it's on us.' I just got really used to my dad being able to work deals."

She laughs at how accustomed they became to being comped.

"Dad was always generous back, but I just didn't know how to buy tickets, do a lot of things like that, because Dad was just the master at getting deals done."

* * * * *

Despite being well known—some might even say famous— the coach wasn't above laughing at himself. Some of his best lines were of the self-deprecating sort.

For instance, when he had emergency surgery in 1997 for a carotid artery blockage, he cracked, "My wife tells me that's why I had them run the ball so much in the Utah game. I wasn't getting enough circulation to my brain."

That was the year the Cougars passed the ball only 16 times in a 20-14 loss to the Utes.

Near the start of the 2000 season, his swan song, Edwards appeared at a press gathering at Cougar Stadium (now LaVell Edwards Stadium), to discuss the upcoming schedule. As he talked, a writer in the audience noticed a mortifying development: Edwards's fly was open.

After the press conference had ended, the writer—a longtime acquaintance—drew Edwards aside and said, "Coach, I just wanted to let you know that while you were up there in front of the media, your fly was unzipped."

The coach turned away and zipped up.

"You know," he chuckled, "the really funny thing about that is this isn't the first time I've done that."

\* \* \* \* \*

The open-fly incident may actually have been symptomatic of a long-held contention that Edwards could be forgetful. Assistant coaches say he sometimes would leave the meeting room to answer the phone and never come back. He had forgotten they were in the middle of a discussion.

Media members would get return calls from Edwards, only to pick up the phone and hear him say, "Uh…um…this is LaVell. I forgot who I was calling."

If he was interrupted by a secretary or colleague during a phone call, he inevitably came back on the line to say, "Now what were we talking about?"

In 2000, BYU held a reunion banquet to commemorate the 1980 Holiday Bowl victory. Former wide receiver Dan Plater's job was to introduce Edwards. The longtime coach showed up in his tuxedo. As Plater, Edwards's wife Patti, and Edwards stood in the portal at the Marriott Center, waiting for their introduction, the coach exclaimed: "Look, I've forgotten my cummerbund."

Patti was horrified. The big night, black tie affair—and the coach forgot his cummerbund.

Plater tried to hold back the laughter.

But in typical Edwards style, he pulled it off. He met the crowd holding his jacket closed.

That's the thing about Edwards. He forgot a lot of things. But he never forgot about being LaVell.

And the fans loved him for it.

\* \* \* \* \*

Edwards's forgetfulness was one of his most endearing qualities—even to those he forgot.

While still the head coach at BYU, Edwards was a popular public speaker. Many of his engagements were LDS Church "fireside" programs designed to inspire youth.

Too bad they didn't inspire him to get out a road map.

In the late 1990s, he was scheduled to speak to a fireside group in Twin Falls, Idaho. BYU associate athletic director Mike King, whose brother was an LDS Church leader in that area, had arranged the engagement.

King's brother called on a Monday morning and said: "Where was LaVell last week? He never made it up here."

King said he didn't know. LaVell was supposed to have been there, on schedule.

Later that day when he saw Edwards, he asked what happened.

"I thought it was in *Idaho* Falls," said Edwards. "I always get Idaho Falls and Twin Falls all screwed up."

Edwards went on to explain that he had driven to Idaho Falls, pulled off the freeway, and looked everywhere he could imagine for the correct address. Finally, he was forced to turn around and drive home.

To his credit, Edwards rescheduled the appearance.

And that time he drove 263 miles in the *right* direction.

\* \* \* \* \*

*When he coached his first game, against Kansas State, all Edwards want-
ed to do was be as successful as the marching band.
(Photo by Mark Philbrick, BYU Photo)*

That wasn't the only time Edwards ended up in the wrong place at the right time.

On another occasion, a neighbor of Edwards's passed away, so the longtime coach decided to pay his respects.

Edwards didn't know the neighbor well, but he drove to the mortuary and stood respectfully in line. When he got to the front of the line, the deceased's wife expressed how grateful and surprised she was that Edwards had come to her husband's viewing. After all, he had been such a big BYU fan.

Edwards, though, was slightly confused.

He didn't recognize the wife.

Didn't recognize the deceased, either.

As he walked out of the funeral home, Edwards realized there had been two funeral viewings at the same mortuary. One line had gone to the left, the other to the right. Edwards had joined the wrong line and paid his respects to a total stranger.

The good news was that it was a BYU fan nonetheless.

The family was duly impressed that the coach of the BYU football team would think enough of a longtime fan to attend his viewing.

\* \* \* \* \*

In 1993, the Cougars played their first-ever game against Notre Dame.

Just before leaving the locker room on game days, Edwards had a tradition of leading the team in a chant. He would call out, for example, "One, two, three: Beat the Rams!" or whatever team they were playing that day.

That year they had been tromped 68-14 by UCLA the previous week. It must have still been on his mind, because when the team gathered in the locker room before taking the field, he shouted,

"OK, guys, One! Two! Three! Beat the Bruins!"

There was an uncomfortable pause.

Then the players called out a rather fragmented, "Beat the

*Edwards knew Lou Holtz, and he knew the Irish...eventually.*
*(Photo by Mark Philbrick, BYU Photo)*

*Irish!*"

Wrong team.

Right attitude.

\* \* \* \* \*

Edwards never changed, no matter how good or bad his teams were.

The Cougars were on their way to a disappointing 6-5 season in 1997. It was only the second time in two decades they didn't reach a bowl game.

Looking for ways to improve, Edwards one day announced they needed to weed out distractions. One of the steps was to discontinue allowing fans to spend too much time with the players on the day before games. Between fans, parents and relatives, the players seemed to be losing focus.

Edwards had someone put up signs in the locker rooms and around the meeting rooms stating the new rules. That was on a Wednesday. On Friday, in Dallas for a game with SMU, King noticed at the team meal that there were some fans in attendance—the same sort they had outlawed earlier in the week.

"What happened?" King said to Edwards. "Who were those people?"

It turned out Edwards had invited them.

Said Edwards sheepishly, "Well, Mike, that was a heck of a rule on Wednesday, but it wasn't worth a damn on Friday."

\* \* \* \* \*

You're never too old to be a kid, especially if you're a football coach.

Edwards had a playful side, and it was never more apparent than the year he decided to celebrate the end of two-a-days with the team.

It was near the end of his career. Edwards had long before begun watching practice from a golf cart, to reduce strain on his back and legs. But it was a team tradition to celebrate the end of fall practices by stretching out a large strip of plastic sheeting onto the field, watering it with a hose, and letting players take a running slide.

That year they decided to enlist Edwards. After considerable cajoling by the players, he finally consented. Backing up, he ran, dived, and slid.

Maybe *bounced* is a better word.

When he got up, he looked as though he had played in the final scrimmage. He had slammed his face on the ground, chipped a tooth and split his lip.

"He starts running, full bore, and it's hilarious. Instead of crouching and pushing off, he jumps into the air like he's going into a swimming pool. He lands midsection first, and absolutely *racks* himself up. Then he hits his face. It was horrible. He stands up crouched over, trying to catch his air, and walks off sort of bow-legged, trying to figure out what happened with his teeth," said former player Hans Olsen. "We're all quiet, but we decide the next year we weren't going to have him slide."

You could say he was slip-sliding away toward retirement.

\* \* \* \* \*

Sometimes you just never know when—or if—it's a good time to laugh.

But Edwards was always there to set the tone.

Rex Lee was a much beloved and respected president of BYU from 1989-96. A former U.S. solicitor general, he was also a big sports fan, who made a practice of attending major football functions. One of those was the annual invitation to a bowl game. Officials from the Holiday Bowl met with school and team representatives to issue an invitation. Someone gave Lee a bowl hat to wear for publicity pictures.

A slender man with a small head, Lee put on the cap.

It was too high, too wide and the brim was way too flat.

It fit him like a traffic cone.

Though players and staff were stifling laughs, not wanting to hurt Lee's feelings, the ceremony proceeded. Edwards was called upon to make a few remarks. When he got to the podium he took one look at Lee and said what everyone else in the room had been thinking: "Nice hat."

There was dead silence for an instant. Then the room burst into loud laughter.

With his timing and humor, Edwards could even get away with teasing the president.

\* \* \* \* \*

Edwards was known as a hands-off coach. He delegated responsibility to his assistants and let them do their work. He was also fairly low-key with the players, letting the assistants do most of the shouting.

But when he did have something to say, it was worthwhile.

One year, wide receiver Chuck Cutler, who went on to become a team captain and record-setting receiver, went out for a quick hitch pass in a game. After catching the ball, he turned and began juking the opponent. Fake left, fake right, stutter-step—everything in his arsenal.

The defense plowed over him anyway.

Cutler reached up and tried to stiff-arm one of the tacklers, but his hand got caught in the facemask.

Soon he was on the sidelines with a dislocated finger. The training staff was quickly in action, twisting the finger, trying to snap it back. Cutler looked up to see Edwards, watching the proceedings.

The coach said nothing about the injury. But he did say something about Cutler's moves.

"Hey, Cutler," he said. "Next time, just make *one* move and run up field."

\* \* \* \* \*

Great coach. Slightly scary driver.

Edwards could talk and chew gum at the same time, no problem. He could drive and chew gum, too.

What he seemed to have a problem with was driving and talking. He would drive one-handed, rest his arm on the back of the seat and look directly at the passenger as he spoke.

Sometimes that gave rise to suspicions he wasn't exactly paying attention to whatever was ahead.

Dick Felt, a former BYU assistant, recalled riding home from Salt Lake with Edwards one afternoon. The freeway had some work being done on the shoulder. Whirring along at just above the speed limit, Edwards, who was driving, was talking to Felt.

Directly to Felt, as a matter of fact.

Suddenly one of the tires slipped off into the shoulder as they passed Point of the Mountain at the border of Salt Lake and Utah counties.

"Remember," said Felt, "LaVell's going 70 miles an hour, he's got his right hand on the back of the seat, his left hand on the steering wheel, and we wandered over."

When the front tire hit the soft shoulder, the car skidded sideways. Traveling at a relatively high speed, Edwards calmly whipped the steering wheel to his left and piloted the car back under control.

Then he went back to talking as though nothing had happened.

*"As I was saying..."*

\* \* \* \* \*

Then there were the low-speed driving problems.

Edwards had a habit of going each morning, after the coaching staff meeting, to a convenience store near the edge of campus for a soft drink. Often other football staffers would meet him at the same store.

One day, in the late 1990s, Chad Bunn, the team's video coordinator, and several other football people were at the store. In walked Edwards.

"I have a problem," began Edwards.

Bunn and others asked how they could help. Edwards led the small group outside the store and pointed to his car. It was high-centered on a concrete parking slab. When he had pulled in to park, he had come in too hard.

"We had to go out there and lift the front of his car over the slab," said Chad Bunn, now BYU's director of video operations.

* * * * *

Edwards was a classic, no doubt about it. So was his pinball game.

So, it could be argued, was his driving.

In the late 1990s, Edwards asked a couple of his players, Hans Olsen and Justin Ena, to help him move a pinball machine. It was a machine he loved—an old relic that had seen its way through his children's growing-up years; now his grandchildren loved playing with it.

The machine was in need of repair, so Edwards arranged to have Olsen and Ena load the machine into a pickup truck and go with him to a repair shop in Orem. On the appointed day, the players arrived.

"Coach," said Olsen, "do you think we should tighten this down?"

"Naw. Don't worry about it," Edwards said.

As Edwards drove the pickup truck west along 800 North in Orem, he had to make a left-hand turn into the parking area of the repair shop. An oncoming car was approaching in the opposite direction. Hoping to avoid waiting, Edwards gunned the accelerator, and the pickup jerked forward as he turned. Out went the pinball machine, soaring through the air and landing on the ground, scattering pieces all over Utah County.

"I'm laughing so hard, and I turn and look at LaVell and he's giving me that face," said Olsen. "So I stop laughing."

Edwards walked to the mangled machine lying in the street. Unperturbed, he said, "Well, we're by the shop anyway. If we were going to break it, this was the place."

The two players jumped out of the vehicle, picked up the machine and carried it into the repair shop. When the repairman looked at the twisted mess, he said, "LaVell, when you explained to me what needed to be fixed, this isn't what I pictured. This might need a few more repairs."

\* \* \* \* \*

Edwards was a great coach. But was he in control of the weather?

Eddie Green thought so.

Green was a player for the Cougars in the late 1980s and early '90s. He was also a person whom Edwards convinced he could control the elements.

The team would be out practicing in the rain, and Edwards would come to the practice field. Sure enough, a few minutes later the rain would stop.

"Coach controls the weather," Green would say.

Some days Edwards would change practice times, telling the players it was going to be snowing or raining at the normal time, so he would move practice up or back.

Sure enough, they always got their practice in.

"Eddie," Edwards would say, "I predict it is going to stop raining today about 3 o'clock and we'll be able to practice after that."

Sure enough, right around 3 p.m., the rain would stop and practice would proceed.

Fact is, Edwards had a friend who worked at the weather station on campus. Each day, the coach would call his friend and ask for the forecast at practice time.

The coach never did tell Eddie Green.

He'd just as soon have him believe Coach E was also in charge of the skies.

\* \* \* \* \*

Many assume Edwards had a grand plan when he became BYU's head coach in 1972. Not so.

He just wanted to be respectable.

One of his former assistant coaches, Mel Olsen, said he heard Edwards say that when he took over the football team, "his

*Even the stoic Edwards became emotional when LDS Church President
Gordon B. Hinckley announced that the stadium would be named after him.
(Photo by Mark Philbrick, BYU Photo)*

dream was to reach the talent level and performance level of the marching band."

\* \* \* \* \*

As ageless as Edwards was, time took its toll. Not necessarily on his coaching ability as much as on his physical capabilities.

As he neared the end of his career, Edwards was often seen bent over on the sidelines during games, legs spread, hands on his knees, looking at the ground. Most fans assumed it was the coach thinking about plays. He was usually thinking about his aching back, and leaning over helped alleviate the pain.

So the next time you're watching a video of some of BYU's great games, and you see the longtime coach hunched over, go ahead and imagine the great mind poring over possible scenarios.

Just keep in mind that he could have been merely thinking of finding a nice, soft place to sit.

# Chapter 2

## *Bowl Games*

Memory will forever credit Jim McMahon with winning the 1980 Holiday Bowl—affectionately known since as the "Miracle Bowl"—thanks to his last-second touchdown pass against Southern Methodist. Yet the game was actually won, 46-45, on an extra-point kick by Kurt Gunther. Not many recall that. Even fewer know it was a kick Gunther was lucky to make.

Gunther wasn't even on scholarship when he made the all-important kick. As a sophomore, he walked on and earned a spot as a non-scholarship player. But the number one kicker, Dave Taylor, was declared ineligible at the last minute.

"They pulled me out of my Stats 101 class and said, 'Get your gear, we need you to kick for us,'" said Gunther.

He was so nervous he forgot his helmet on his first road trip. BYU was playing at New Mexico in the season opener, and he didn't realize his mistake until he got to Albuquerque.

One of the BYU assistant coaches had a friend who owned a private jet. The coach called and asked him to drop by the football office, pick up Gunther's helmet, and fly it to the Duke City.

"I was so excited just to be the starting kicker," said Gunther. He was living at home in Provo and paying his own tuition at the time.

That, of course, changed the moment he made the kick that beat SMU. Coach LaVell Edwards was so grateful, he put Gunther on scholarship the next two years, plus a third that after Gunther had used up his eligibility but was still working on his accounting degree.

Although Gunther was a reliable kicker for the Cougars

through three seasons, the one against SMU was the kick of his life. Not only did it provide BYU with its first-ever bowl win, but it allayed fears that the Cougars couldn't win on a kick. The previous year, BYU was in position to win against Indiana in the closing moments, but Brent Johnson—a normally fine kicker, as well—pulled his head up and missed a 27-yard field goal that would have won the game.

After McMahon completed the "Hail Mary" pass that tied the 1980 bowl game, the stadium was in an uproar. The play ranks with one of the most amazing in college football history.

"Everyone was celebrating, with the exception of two people," said Gunther. "That was LaVell and McMahon, because they both knew darn well we had to make the PAT to win."

Bill Schoepflin, who moments earlier had blocked a SMU kick to set up the game-tying pass, was Gunther's holder. He called out the count: "Blue 13." That confirmed Gunther would kick the PAT and that it wouldn't be a fake kick. But when Schoepflin raised his hand to take the snap, the ball didn't come.

Earlier in the game, Corey Pace had snapped one over punter Clay Brown's head. He was nervous and tentative.

"I talked to him later and I said, 'Corey, we practiced that play a million times. Why didn't you snap it in time?'" said Gunther. "He said, 'Kurt, I was so scared that when I bent over and grabbed the ball, my knees were almost hitting each other.'"

So when Schoepflin raised his hand, Gunther began leaning forward to go into his kicking motion.

Still no snap.

"I lean and I lean and I lean," recalled Gunther. "The ball doesn't come. So I have to take a stutter-step. I throw my left foot in front of me to keep from falling on my face. Then, finally, the ball comes."

But the scare wasn't over.

Gunther was using a one-inch tee for field goals. When Schoepflin fielded the snap, he accidentally placed the ball on the corner of the tee so that it was resting half on the grass.

Not a good situation in no-pressure conditions, but a horrible situation when it's the game winner.

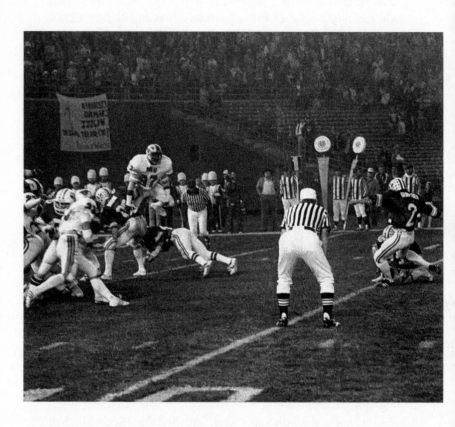

*Kurt Gunther's historic kick, by all rights, shouldn't have gone through the uprights.*
*(Photo by Mark Philbrick, BYU Photo)*

When Gunther followed through, he lofted a slightly soft, flat kick. It wasn't pretty. It wasn't even average-looking. But it was good nonetheless. The ball went over the crossbar and the Cougars had the win.

After the play, Gunther's best friend from high school leaped the fence and raced past security to tackle him.

"Every week, 22 years later, I have someone tell me their story of whether they left the game or stayed. Just last week, a guy said he broke his chandelier when he leaped into the air," Gunther said.

Another fan broke his hand when in jubilation he struck the end of his couch. One BYU enthusiast claims to have driven off the road near Santaquin, Utah as he listened on the radio, crashing his Cadillac into some bushes.

Such are the memories of the greatest moments, frozen in time—the foggy night, the chilly air, the thrill of the unexpected.

Anyone who follows BYU football remembers where he or she was when the news came that the Cougars had won. Gunther remembers, too.

Said Gunther: "I still get goosebumps just talking about it."

* * * * *

There are dreams and then there are dreams.

And no dream was more eerily prophetic than the one Clay Brown's wife had.

The year was 1979, and the Cougars were in the Holiday Bowl. The night before the game against Indiana, she dreamt her husband made the winning catch on the last play of the game.

That, of course, didn't happen, as Indiana went on to beat the Cougars 38-37.

Fortuitously enough, Brown's wife never forgot her dream. The following year, the Cougars were back in the same hotel in the same city for the same bowl game—this time for the legendary "Miracle Bowl" game against Southern Methodist. That year, Brown *did* make the tying catch on McMahon's Hail Mary pass as the clock expired.

As Brown left to go to the stadium that afternoon, he paused before leaving the room and asked his wife, "Remember that dream you had last year?"

She indicated she did.

Said Brown, "Maybe this time."

* * * * *

Fewer than four minutes remaining, a 20-point deficit.

Even now, more than three decades after BYU's improbable bowl win over Southern Methodist, it stands as one of the greatest comebacks in football history.

It was BYU's third trip to the Holiday Bowl, the previous two being close losses to Navy and Indiana. With moments left, history seemed destined to repeat.

That fact wasn't lost on the press contingent at Jack Murphy Stadium in San Diego that night. Most of the writers were well into their game stories, some nearly finished, when BYU began its comeback.

When McMahon completed the game-tying pass as time ran out, and Gunther nailed the game-winning kick, more than one writer had his head in his hands, realizing the game story would have to be rewritten on a tight deadline. One Texas writer who was all but finished (albeit prematurely) sat with his head on the press table, pounding his fist.

Others hadn't written their entire stories, but had mapped out their plans on game coverage. Some had begun planning to write about BYU's history of bowl-game futility.

At least one writer didn't mind a change of plans, though. Marion Dunn, of Provo's *Daily Herald*, had covered the Cougars for years. A well-known writer in Utah, Dunn made it no secret he loved seeing the Cougars win.

Thus, he sat quietly through most of the game, watching events unfold—until the final pass.

When McMahon found Brown to tie the score, most of those who remained in the stadium erupted in screams. Amid the uproar, Dunn stood in disbelief, then shouted to no one in particular, "Take that, Texas!"

\* \* \* \* \*

It will probably surprise no one to learn the night before the Cougars won the "Miracle Bowl," Jim McMahon was out late.

Real late.

On the good side, he wasn't touring the nightclubs of San Diego. On the bad side, he didn't go to bed until around 5 a.m. anyway.

McMahon was friends with fellow quarterbacks Ryan Tibbitts, a senior, and sophomore Gym Kimball. They were in a nearby room at their hotel the Mission Bay Hilton.

About 12:30 a.m. Kimball and Tibbitts heard a knock on the door. There stood McMahon. "Can I hang out in your room?" he asked.

They ended up talking most of the night. Just before sunrise, McMahon left for his room and slept until the team met late that morning.

Ah, to be 21 years old again, when you don't need to sleep.

And you're still at your best the next day.

\* \* \* \* \*

It has been well chronicled how McMahon refused to come off the field on a fourth-down play with under eight minutes remaining and BYU trailing by 19 points.

Edwards, who was standing next to offensive coordinator Doug Scovil, had ordered the punting team onto the field. Everyone came off but McMahon.

This is how the conversation went, according to Tibbitts, who was standing next to the coaches at that moment:

Coaches: "Jim, get off the field, the punting team is going in!"

McMahon didn't budge.

Coaches: "Jim, GET OFF THE FIELD! The punting team is going in."

No movement on McMahon's part.

Finally, Edwards called a timeout, fearing a delay-of-game penalty. McMahon came to the sidelines, where he faced the two coaches.

"Are we just going to [expletive] quit?" he yelled.

The coaches said they weren't quitting, just punting.

To which McMahon replied, "If we punt, I've played my last down in a BYU uniform!"

The coaches reneged, pulling the punting unit. McMahon threw to Brown for a first down, then completed five of the next six passes. BYU scored on the drive and went on to win.

"So," said Tibbitts, "the 'miracle finish' started with an obscenity."

\* \* \* \* \*

Tibbitts laughs at how the final minutes of that Holiday Bowl unfolded.

In the locker room, moments after the game, equipment manager Floyd Johnson—a missionary-minded member of the LDS Church—said, "If *that* doesn't give you a testimony [of divine intervention], I don't know what would!"

Tibbitts points out that the player who blocked the punt that set up the winning touchdown, Bill Schoepflin, was a Catholic. Matt Braga, who caught one of BYU's fourth-quarter touchdowns was too.

Likewise for McMahon and Brown, who combined for the final touchdown.

"I always say in the battle between the Mormons and the Methodists, the Catholics won," said Tibbitts.

At one subsequent speaking engagement, Tibbitts told the story, which drew a laugh. Not to be outdone, Edwards stood for his remarks and said, "Ryan forgets Kurt Gunther made the kick. So it was a [Mormon] returned missionary who won it!"

Said Gunther, "LaVell tells me that story every time he sees me."

\* \* \* \* \*

It is one of the enduring images of BYU football history—the "Miracle Bowl" just finished, players and fans going mad, Edwards in complete shock.

BYU's comeback was indeed shocking. Asked to comment on the final pass from McMahon to Brown by a television reporter, Edwards stammered. He was nearly speechless. There were two possible reasons for that. One, he was indeed surprised. Two, there was Mel Farr's knee.

Farr was a team equipment manager for years, and he had a tendency to get highly enthused.

After McMahon threw the game-tying pass and the extra-point kick was ruled good, confusion reigned. What fans don't know is that just before the TV reporter caught up with Edwards for his comment, Farr raced after Edwards and leaped into his arms. As he came up, his knee caught Edwards in the midsection—or possibly somewhere south of there.

Ouch.

Edwards said that isn't what happened. Former video coordinator Chad Bunn claimed he has the evidence on film.

So if it appeared at first glance that Edwards was speechless about the improbable win, he was.

Perhaps for more than one reason.

* * * * *

The true sign of a great leader: being able to call a good audible.

In that regard, former BYU president Jeffrey R. Holland ranks with the greats.

Holland had watched along with everyone else as BYU fell steadily behind at Holiday Bowl III. Like many others, when the deficit fell to 20 points with under four minutes remaining, he felt resigned to the fact the Cougars would lose yet another bowl game.

He told the publicity people he was leaving the press box early so he could be in the locker room to speak to the players. The game was over. It was time for words of consolation.

*Edwards and president Jeffrey Holland were two guys it paid to stay close to.*
*(Photo by Mark Philbrick, BYU Photo)*

Waiting under the stands, near the locker rooms, he heard roaring from above. Out of curiosity, he walked out onto the field. Upon seeing the celebration, he realized what had happened—the Cougars had come back to win.

Expecting to deliver a talk about fortitude, character and adversity, he was now in charge of giving a victory talk.

Not a bad option.

Nobody recalls exactly what was said. But this much most of the players will remember. Holland said, "I have had some great heroes in my life," listing some of history's leaders. "I've just added another name to my list of heroes: The 1980 BYU football team!"

Nice audible.

Delivering an unrehearsed talk was never more welcome.

\* \* \* \* \*

In the waning minutes of the game against SMU, the Cougars completed an onside kick. The play jumpstarted them and led to a touchdown and two-point conversion that put BYU in striking distance.

It was a huge play, a timely moment. Todd Shell, who went on to play in the NFL, made the recovery.

Or so the record states.

Actually, it was Tom Holmoe who made the recovery. Holmoe, who was also on the kickoff unit for that play, says Schell has gladly taken credit for that play for over 22 years.

"We have a thing going about that play to this day," said Holmoe.

When the kick was initiated, the teams piled on the ball. According to Holmoe, he came up with the recovery. But at the bottom of the pile, he could feel SMU players "scratching, kicking and biting, and the referees aren't saying anything."

Finally, a referee blew his whistle and called possession to BYU. Holmoe let go of the ball and scrambled out of the pile. But Shell, who was still in the confusion, grabbed the ball, just to be sure, and clutched it.

When he emerged holding the prize, statisticians in the press box assumed it was Shell who recovered. They duly noted it in the official statistics and on the play-by-play chart.

A short time later, a rally was held at the Marriott Center in Provo, where thousands of BYU fans showed up to honor the team's victory. Players were interviewed about the big plays of the game. "Todd just picked it up from there," said Holmoe. "They interviewed me, and I was saying I recovered the fumble, he stole my glory," Holmoe adds.

But the papers the day after the game said it was Shell. So did the stat sheets. Holmoe had only his word.

"Now Todd is like, 'I don't remember that. I recovered the ball,'" laughed Holmoe.

Ever hear of the term *carpe diem?*

\* \* \* \* \*

The Cougars' first trip to the Liberty Bowl was in 1998 to play Tulane. Among the non-game functions was the obligatory homage to Elvis Presley. Most of the Cougar team toured Graceland, the former Elvis home and now a major tourist trap in Memphis.

Quarterback Kevin Feterik loved the place, raving about its tacky '70s style. His favorite room was the "Jungle Room," which was decorated with shag carpet and jungle-themed furniture.

Said Feterik: "I wish I could live in it right now."

Teammate Daren Yancey was also impressed, telling a couple of *Deseret News* reporters, "I never realized how extensive his records were and how great he was. I walked into that hall and saw the gold records and said, 'That was his? That's his? Holy cow! He really is the King!' I had no idea how extensive his work was."

Meanwhile, All-America linebacker Rob Morris stopped at the gravesite of the King of Rock 'n' Roll and—mostly for effect—kissed the marker.

Said Morris, "Everyone is an Elvis fan."

\* \* \* \* \*

Well, almost everyone.

Edwards made the tour but shed nary a tear for the King of Rock and Roll.

"I never was an Elvis fan," he said.

Edwards said he never even liked the Beatles until they were gone. His style leaned toward Frank Sinatra, Vic Damone, Tony Bennett and Andy Williams.

As for the music his players listened to, he wasn't convinced of the benefits of rap or hip-hop, either.

"No. No. They haven't sold me on those," he told the *News.* "Nor will they."

\* \* \* \* \*

OK, it was Christmas Day. Not the most convenient time to play a bowl game.

But in 1992, the Cougars couldn't be choosy. They finished the regular season just 7-5. Still, they had tied for the WAC championship, so the question was merely where they would end up.

It turned out to be Honolulu for the Aloha Bowl.

Who knew getting to the Islands could be such a pain?

The charter airline the Cougars used for the game was a good one. At least good enough that one of its main contracts was with the U.S. military. That didn't exactly help the Cougars' cause. The team arrived at the airport in midmorning to fly to Hawaii the week of the game, only to end up waiting…and waiting.

As the team buses sat on the tarmac, it became clear something had gone wrong. A few minutes stretched into an hour, then two, then three. Next, the explanations began coming in. Because the military used the charter line, it had requested the plane the Cougars had intended to take to Hawaii. That delayed their departure a few hours. When the plane finally did land, it took an excruciatingly long time to load on the food. Somehow, a double order of food had been received, which wasn't a problem with the Cougar players. The trouble was, the airline didn't have room to store it all.

Then there was a problem with the water in the bathrooms, which needed to be remedied.

The team didn't finally get in the air until the wee hours of the next morning.

On top of that, a late summer volcano eruption in Alaska had occurred. Consequently, flights to the Islands were diverted to steer clear of residual pollution and avoid the risk of another eruption.

Eventually the team arrived in Honolulu about 6:30 a.m., a day late. That ruined the team's schedule for that day.

BYU players ended up sleeping most of the time and losing a day's practice, thanks to the confluence of conditions. When the game arrived, Kansas kicked a field goal with 2:47 remaining to give the Jayhawks a 23-20 victory.

Seemed to the Cougars like a lot of trouble just to lose.

* * * * *

File this one with the Department of Inspiration.

The 1996 BYU Cougars were headed to the Cotton Bowl, on track to complete the longest season in college football history—15 games.

That year, one of the team leaders was undersized, overachieving linebacker Shay Muirbrook.

Even though the Cougars were 13-1 at the time, few BYU fans, or even players, seemed to think they had a chance to beat favored Kansas State. The game would feature a large (40,000-plus) and boisterous KSU fan following.

During the week prior to the game, Edwards closed practice with a talk to his players. Just as his remarks were winding down, Muirbrook interrupted and said, "Coach, I've got something to say."

Edwards told him to go ahead and speak his mind.

"I'm so tired of everyone telling us we can't win. If the players don't believe, no one else is going to believe. I'm here to tell you we're going to win. I'm a senior. We've already won 13 games. So anyone here that doesn't believe we will win might as well go home now!"

Duane Busby, the team's football operations director, was at the gathering.

"From that point on," said Busby, "the whole emotion of the team changed dramatically. By the time the next two practices were over, everyone on the team felt the same."

Muirbrook repeated his challenge when the team went into the locker room after warmups. KSU fans had been chanting, "Overrated! Overrated!" at the Cougars.

As it turned out, BYU won 19-15. Muirbrook was the game's defensive MVP, making six sacks.

"It was one of those rare times," said Busby, "when you see someone's personal convictions so strong that it takes over the whole organization. It really elevated everyone into believing we could beat Kansas State."

Moral to the story: If you're tired of hearing a criticism, do something about it.

# Chapter 3

## *Legendary Plays*

It wasn't exactly a legendary "play." Nor was it particularly inspiring. But it was different.

The year 1980 will always be remembered as the year BYU won its first bowl game. But it will also be remembered for one of the most bizarre incidents in college football history.

In the second half of a game between BYU and Utah State, in Logan on October 18, the Cougars were well on their way to a 70-46 victory. Throughout the game, both teams had been trash-talking one another. Meanwhile, there had been a number of questionable calls and no-calls by the officials.

As the players began to huddle after one play, chaos erupted. A gasp went up from the crowd. Junior Filiaga, a Cougar defensive lineman was suddenly pummeling an official about the head and arms.

Players rushed to pull Filiaga off the official. He was tossed from the game and later suspended.

What instigated the attack? Some at the time said an official used a racial slur. That contention was backed up by at least one source who was on the sidelines and says he overheard the conversation that day.

Others, though, say the impetus wasn't what an official said, but a series of no-calls, combined with constant bickering among players. Whatever the case, all involved were fortunate the incident didn't escalate.

"I remember thinking we were dead," said former backup quarterback Ryan Tibbitts, who was on the sidelines that day. "I had put on my helmet and strapped on the chin strap. I thought the fans would come down after us."

LaVell Edwards says he still doesn't know what happened. His recollection is that Filiaga was upset over being held on several plays, not something an official said.

Edwards said he heard—after the fact—that when Filiaga came to the sidelines, he was still wild-eyed with rage. He was swinging his arms and came close to connecting with roughneck assistant coach Fred Whittingham.

Whittingham grabbed Filiaga by the jersey and growled, "You've already made one stupid mistake today. Don't make another!"

After the game, players provided Filiaga with moral support. A particular vote of confidence came from another defensive lineman who told teammates: "I'm glad Junior hit him, because if he hadn't, I would have."

\* \* \* \* \*

Garth Hall, an assistant coach for the Cougars in 1980, was working from the coaches' booth in the press box the day Filiaga went berserk. He wasn't watching Filiaga specifically, but soon realized something was wrong.

"Junior leaves the huddle and just goes after him," said Hall. "The referee was 10 yards away from him and couldn't see him coming. He probably didn't know at first what hit him."

Hall recalled moaning aloud after it happened.

Filiaga was a pariah in college football circles for a few weeks. Ironically, some say he was one of the most sweet-tempered of the Cougars most of the time.

"The sad part of all that is that there was no more tender guy than Junior," said Hall. "He could be a warrior, but off the field he was the kindest, gentlest kind of person."

Hall added, "I remember saying to myself, 'Not him!' You might expect that out of a jerk, but not Junior."

\* \* \* \* \*

The famous Jim McMahon-to-Clay Brown pass at the end of Holiday Bowl III was indeed a rare occurrence. Brown had to

*Top row, left to right, assistant coaches: Garth Hall, Mel Olsen, Roger French, Mike Holmgren, Norm Chow. Kneeling: Tom Ramage, Dick Felt, Ken Schmidt. (Photo by Mark Philbrick, BYU Photo)*

snare the ball from the grasp of three defenders who converged on him on the final play.

In a sense, credit for the play belongs to a sport other than football—hoops.

When Brown went up for the game-saving catch, he was squared up, facing McMahon upfield. With coverage all about him, Brown braced, bent his knees, spread his legs wide, blocked out with his elbows and went up to grab the ball, just like a power forward going for a rebound.

"At BYU we play a lot of pickup basketball," said reserve quarterback Ryan Tibbitts to the *Rexburg* (ID) *Standard-Journal.* "I've played with Clay and he's a tough rebounder. He's big and strong on the boards. So in the [Holiday Bowl] game, the three or four defensive backs jumped up, and he came down with the ball."

Which brings up an interesting question: How come nobody asked him to try out for basketball?

\* \* \* \* \*

McMahon's "Hail Mary" pass was a last-second effort.

But not the only one.

Others, too, turned in clutch performances in the moment of truth.

On the final play, the blocking scheme required McMahon to set up 10-12 yards from scrimmage. Ray Linford, a tackle on that 1980 team, had it all down pat.

Trouble was, when McMahon took the snap he dropped back about 15 yards, not 10.

Normally the line will block the rushers back to where the quarterback is, and begin "rounding" them out, so they slip past. But because McMahon set up farther back than usual, when Linford began rounding his man he nearly ran him right into the quarterback.

"When I looked back," said Linford, "I saw that Jim had dropped back 15 yards or so. So I leaned on my guy's hip and rode him back."

As it turned out, McMahon got off the pass and the Cougars

won one of the most miraculous games in NCAA history.

"If McMahon had let go of the ball one second later, my guy would have nailed him," says Linford. "He almost got out around me."

Appropriately enough, Linford never did talk to McMahon about the near miss. Perhaps that's the plight of the offensive lineman—to never be noticed.

"He never did say anything to me," said Linford. "He probably didn't even know it happened."

\* \* \* \* \*

It was a crazy play, maybe even weird. It was just what the Missouri Tigers didn't expect.

It wasn't what Edwards expected, either.

For all his scrambling ability, Steve Young was still a quarterback—which meant you could expect him to pass, pitch, hand off or run all the time. Unbeknownst to Missouri, he had one other item on his resume: receiver.

The 1983 Cougars were ranked in the Top 10 going into the Holiday Bowl, having lost only once, 40-36, to Baylor in the season opener.

With time running out against Missouri, trailing 17-14, BYU mounted a stand that gave it the ball on its own six-yard line. Moving to the Tigers' 15 with less than a minute to go, the team huddled. In the press box, offensive coordinator Norm Chow was preparing to call a play.

It was risky. Chow knew it was a play Edwards wouldn't like. But he called the halfback pass anyway.

"Dumbest call I've ever seen," Edwards later kidded Chow.

Running back Eddie Stinnett took a handoff from Young and faked a sweep right, then threw cross-field to Young, who took the ball into the end zone with the winning touchdown. The pass was wobbly and barely cleared the outstretched arms of Missouri's Bobby Bell. Young narrowly caught the pass on his fingertips.

"When it unfolded," said Edwards, "I thought, 'Oh *brother!*'"

On the same play, a BYU receiver charged into the back of a

Missouri defensive back, which should have been a penalty. But none of the officials caught it.

So the Cougars won the game on a trick play. It was smooth, entertaining and perfectly executed, right?

Oh *brother*.

\* \* \* \* \*

Other key plays in BYU history weren't nearly so high profile, and only those close to the action would even remember.

During the 1980 Holiday Bowl, McMahon's "Hail Mary" pass got all the attention. But another play was so critical that the Cougars may not have won without it.

Southern Methodist had forced the Cougars near their own end zone early in the game. McMahon took the snap and rolled to the left, dropping back into the end zone. With a SMU defender bearing down on him, he leaped, cocking the ball at the same time.

As the player struck, McMahon used the opponent's momentum to jackknife his torso forward and snap the ball off in a hard pass. The speed of the throw made certain the pass was completed and the Cougars moved out of range of a safety.

As it turned out, that was two points the Cougars couldn't have afforded to give up, and a play that has been all but forgotten in the mists of time.

\* \* \* \* \*

Quarterback Marc Wilson knew the game, and he always he knew where he was.

In fact, he knew where everyone was.

In a 1979 game against Long Beach State, Wilson was under heavy pressure. Running diagonally to the left, he threw right, just over the outstretched hands of two large defensive linemen. BYU's tight end caught the ball on the run for a large gain. No big deal.

Yet when someone asked Wilson if it was a lucky throw, or if he knew where his tight end was and if he'd be open, Wilson explained it thusly: He knew where the free safety was. If the tight

*Marc Wilson was a quarterback who always knew where his teammates were.*
*(Photo by Mark Philbrick, BYU Photo)*

end was doing his job, he would be cutting across the field, where there would be no one to defend.

"The free safety left the area," said Wilson. "And the cornerback should have rolled with the play, leaving no one to guard the tight end. If he did his job, I knew he should be there."

So that's what goes into being a great quarterback. It's all about knowing where you should be.

Equally important is knowing where everyone else should be.

\* \* \* \* \*

One play.

Dick Felt, the late BYU defensive backfield coach, isn't one to overstate things. Few games, he says, are won or lost—much less seasons—on one play.

But this one was different.

In BYU football annals, most of the famous plays were on the offensive side. Everyone remembers McMahon's Hail Mary pass. Most recall Young's reception in the 1983 Holiday Bowl.

But there is one defensive play that stands out.

Hawaii was threatening to upset BYU in 1984, which really wasn't much of a surprise. Hawaii had often played well against BYU. In part, that's because BYU always recruited well in the Islands—a source of irritation to those who lived there and watched Hawaii football. Second, Hawaii fans never liked the fact that thousands of BYU fans would show up each year for the game in the Islands wearing blue.

So it wasn't exactly a social gathering whenever the teams met.

The Cougars were leading 12-10 with just over 10 minutes left in the game. The Rainbow Warriors had gained a first-and-goal at the BYU two-yard line.

Scouting reports had said Hawaii quarterback Raphel Cherry liked to sneak when close to the goal line, and that proved true. He tried a sneak, for a gain of inches. Next play, a dive to the left side of the line. Same results. It was third down and just inches to the goal line.

BYU free safety Kyle Morrell crept near scrimmage as Cherry was calling the count. After hearing him call signals in previous series, Morrell knew the cadence. He took a step back and leaped, clearing scrimmage almost simultaneously as the ball was snapped.

Morrell hurtled over Cherry and caught him by the back collar, coming down head first, *behind* him, and pulling him down. Hawaii settled for a field goal and a 13-12 lead with 10:02 remaining. BYU went on to win 18-13.

"I swear—and I've said this before—I think a professional football team could line up and go 100 repetitions, and I don't think they could ever get a play done like that," said Felt. "Nobody could. I don't think you could duplicate that."

After making the play, Morrell came to the sidelines.

"I'm gonna tell everyone I called that," said Felt.

When asked why he decided to make the gamble, Morrell replied, "We had to make a play. I had nothing to lose."

It was one of the most spectacular plays in Cougar history. Not a single official even reached for a flag. The timing and positioning were perfect.

BYU continued undefeated the remaining nine games to claim its only national championship.

"You can seldom say a single play won a football game. Or maybe in one game or situation it makes the difference. But that *was* the national championship, that one play," said Felt. "If Hawaii had beaten us, we never would have been in the position in the polls to be where we ended up."

\* \* \* \* \*

Most BYU fans are idealistic. Some are skeptical. A handful are flat-out naïve.

For those in the latter category, stop reading here.

This is a story that flies in the face of the "everyone's-a-brother" theory.

Although BYU was widely known for its coaching staff stability during the LaVell Edwards era, there was one incident that pretty much lay waste to the idea that they always got along famously.

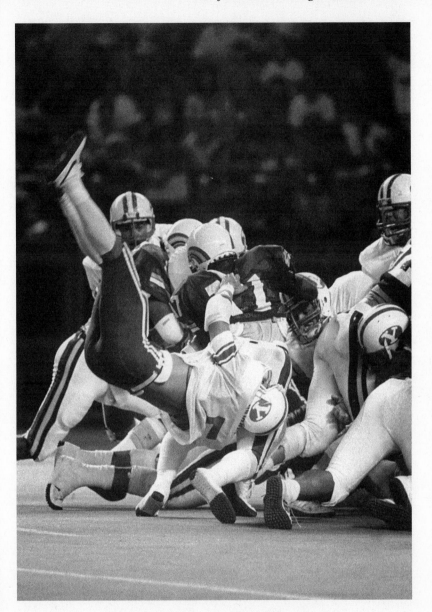

*Some say Kyle Morrell's tackle of Hawaii's Raphel
Cherry triggered the title run in 1984.
(Photo by Mark Philbrick, BYU Photo)*

In the early 1980s, the Cougars were competing in Logan against Utah State. Several of the Cougar coaching staff sat in the press box, scouting the game from above and relaying suggestions via headset to Edwards on the sidelines. Sometimes in the cramped press box booth at Romney Stadium, the temperature rose to uncomfortable levels—and it had nothing to do with the cramped quarters.

The game had gone as expected, but in one situation, Hall, then serving as a running backs coach, had a suggestion. But Chow, the quarterbacks coach, wasn't going along. He had a better idea. At least that's what he thought.

Before long, they began to argue.

And there wasn't much room for arguing in the tiny booth.

Suddenly Chow reached over and angrily smacked Hall in the face. It appeared it could have escalated into an all-out fistfight. That's when Felt reached in and separated the two.

"I've often thought in my own mind that there are two coaching styles," said Felt. "There are Type A and Type B coaches. Type A coaches are the dictator-type head coaches, the type of coach who runs everything and is ornery and hard to deal with, so his assistant coaches band together against the head coach.

"The Type B coach is more laid back and lets the assistants make decisions. That's the type LaVell was. He would never do anything like being a dictator, so the tendency with Type B coaches is that the assistants will banter with each other. That might be what happened there. And yet they were all so respectful of LaVell."

Though the coaches calmed down after the incident, soon everyone on the team knew of the spat.

As with the Filiaga story, it wasn't technically a legendary play.

But it did become a legendary story.

* * * * *

For anyone who was there, there is no doubt.

For anyone who heard the sound, it's not even a question.

Greatest hit ever made by a BYU player? Kurt Gouveia's tackle on Hawaii's Walter Murray in 1985, hands down.

Second-greatest hit? Same thing—the first time around.

The final regular season game was at Hawaii and the Rainbow Warriors were talking. That year, Hawaii was promoting Murray for postseason honors. He was lean and fast, a highly regarded NFL prospect.

During that game, Gouveia, a BYU linebacker, had been getting razzed by fans, which didn't sit well with him. He wasn't the submissive type.

"As mean and nasty a player as you ever want to know," said former quarterback Blaine Fowler.

Not surprisingly, when Murray came over the middle on a route, Gouveia was there to make the stop—and then some. He caught Murray hard in the numbers, sprawling him flat on the turf.

The crowd gasped. Gouveia climbed off.

Murray, though, bounced up, trash-talking Gouveia.

A few plays later, Hawaii then made its big mistake: Same play, same route.

Same result, too. Murray ran across the middle, Gouveia was there to meet him.

That time Murray didn't get up.

The second time, Gouveia caught him hard, his helmet connecting with Murray at chin-level. Gouveia flattened him so hard on the second try, the first thing to hit the ground was the top of Murray's helmet.

He was out cold.

Gouveia didn't do a victory dance or jump up and down. He just straddled Murray for a second. Then he made a slight motion with his hand that seemed to say, "There you go, you asked for it," and walked away.

"Hardest hit I've ever seen," concluded former BYU assistant coach Tom Ramage. "Murray didn't get up. He was *out.*"

Added Fowler, "It was one of those hits that even as football players we just went '*Ohhhhhh!* That was nasty!'"

\* \* \* \* \*

There was Danny "Pluto" Plater. And Glen "Koz" Kozlowski. And, of course, Roger "The Creature" French.

Good nicknames, one and all.

But one of the best nicknames ever at BYU? That would belong to Steve "Wrong Way" Corson.

Corson only lettered at BYU for one year. Unfortunately, he is best remembered for a play that sets coaches teeth on edge.

The play came on a series in which Corson was sent in as part of the punt return team. The opposing team punted the ball, which bounced on the 15-yard line and appeared headed for the end zone. But Corson, who had played both directions during the year, got confused and apparently thought he was on the punting team. Instead of letting the ball roll into the end zone for a touchback, he raced after it and leaped to bat it back out of the end zone. The opposition recovered the ball on BYU's one-yard line.

Right play. Wrong situation.

Hence, "Wrong Way" Corson.

\* \* \* \* \*

Kickers often get overlooked. Unless they are attempting the final play of the game, they largely go unnoticed.

But Lee Johnson got noticed. Always.

Johnson played at BYU from 1981-84, before embarking on a long NFL career. In college he kicked barefoot. His kicking was so prolific, he would stop traffic—at least the kind that was on the football field.

"The whole team would just stop and watch in practice," said Fowler. "I can imagine how hard it would be just going out and trying to catch a punt. They were spinning the opposite direction [he was left-footed] and it would come down with the nose straight down. You can break a hand like that."

Another former QB, Robbie Bosco agreed. "We would be doing drills and he would punt and we'd all stop throwing and watch." Players would try to measure how high Johnson's punts would go by looking at the angle against the Wasatch Mountains that skirted the stadium.

"We'd count the hang time. It was incredible," said Bosco.

To this day, Bosco maintains he saw Johnson execute the greatest punt he has ever seen.

BYU played Baylor in the second game of 1984. The Cougars were coming off their surprise season-opening win over Pittsburgh.

On one down, the Cougars were backed deep into their own territory. So far, in fact, that when Johnson went in to punt, he was in the BYU end zone. The snap came and Johnson kicked.

"It took off like a rocket," said Bosco. "The ball landed on the other 20 yard-line. He kicked it 80 yards in the air. I couldn't believe it. I'd never seen anything like it.

"That was the most impressive punt I have ever seen at any level, any time."

# Chapter 4

## *Gary Crowton*

In early 2000, the rumors had begun. LaVell Edwards had not yet publicly announced it would be his final season, but Cougar administrators already knew. So it was imperative that they begin looking for a replacement.

One plan was to hire Gary Crowton—an assistant coach with the Chicago Bears—as Edwards's offensive coordinator for the 2000 season, then slide him into the top spot when Edwards retired. Norm Chow had just left to take a job at North Carolina State, leaving a position open.

"We called Gary in January or February," said Val Hale, BYU's former director of athletics. "And he was a little reluctant to even be talking with us, but he agreed. But it had to be handled delicately. So I called the Bears to get permission to talk to Gary. We agreed this had to be extremely confidential, because it could hurt both parties if this got out."

BYU arranged to fly Crowton to Utah for interviews. All prospective BYU coaches are required to meet with school administrators and LDS Church general authorities. On the day Crowton arrived, Hale drove to Salt Lake International Airport to pick him up. They had agreed to meet at the curb to avoid attracting attention.

Crowton was immediately taken to the LDS Church Office Building for interviews. They drove into the basement parking lot and took a downstairs entrance to the building, remaining as low profile as possible.

"So we're sitting there, waiting to go upstairs with security," continued Hale, "and in walks this woman who says, 'Gary! What are *you* doing here?'"

It was Crowton's cousin.

So much for secrecy.

After small talk—and not a little perspiring—the party made its way up to meet with several LDS general authorities. Hale then took Crowton to a barbecue restaurant in nearby Midvale, before driving to Provo. For the next couple of days, Crowton met with BYU leaders. He left town on a Thursday.

Early the next week, Dick Harmon, then with the Provo *Daily Herald,* and now a writer at the *Deseret Morning News* in Salt Lake, called Hale.

"Val, I hear Crowton was in town over the weekend," said Harmon.

"He was?" said Hale. "That's news to me. I didn't talk to him this weekend."

Hale laughs now, saying Crowton left on a Thursday, which means he technically wasn't in town *over the weekend.*

As it turned out, Crowton didn't come to Provo for the 2000 season, anyway. But by the time Edwards retired, Crowton had already done all his interviews. It was simply a matter of making a decision as to who would succeed the legend.

\* \* \* \* \*

Sometimes you keep those types of things quiet, other times you don't.

In early December of 2000, BYU had decided to go with Crowton as the new head coach. The school wanted to quietly fly Crowton into town and have a formal press conference to make the announcement. He was to be picked up in a private plane and flown to Utah.

But to Hale's chagrin, the story of Crowton's upcoming visit was in the newspapers before the announcement was made.

How did the word leak out?

Hale believed a pilot of the plane sent to pick up Crowton had mentioned to his father that he was going to Chicago to pick up the new BYU football coach. His father, an avid BYU fan, then

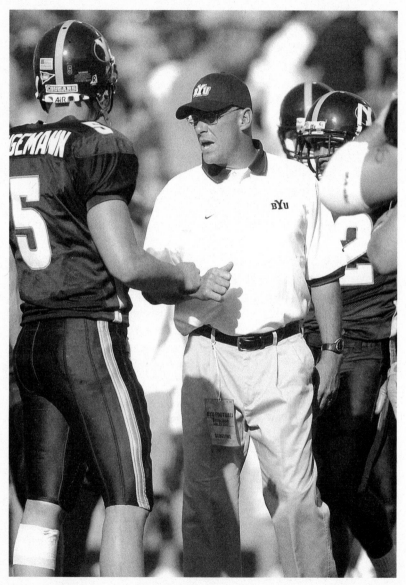

*Gary Crowton made it clear from the start that he wanted players to sit up and listen.*
*(Photo by Mark Philbrick, BYU Photo)*

went to church on Sunday and announced that Gary Crowton was to become the new BYU coach to his LDS priesthood group.

"From there it went to the Internet, then to talk radio and it's all over," Hale remembered.

Want to get the word out on anything?

Tell someone at church.

\* \* \* \* \*

Other times—mysteriously—not many people find out.

Such was the case with Andy Reid.

Though the current Kansas City Chiefs head coach took himself out of the running for the BYU job, he met with school officials long before his name appeared in the newspapers. Oddly enough, the media never found out about it.

Hale says one of the first people BYU interviewed to succeed Edwards was Reid, a former Cougar player. BYU officials flew to Phoenix to talk to Reid, whose team was playing the Arizona Cardinals that weekend. They met Reid and his wife in a Phoenix hotel room in October of 2000, during Edwards's final season. (They also met with former Arizona State and Dallas Cowboys quarterback Danny White on the trip.)

As the party came down to the hotel lobby together, they got off the elevator and, to their surprise, ran into Eagles tight end and former BYU star Chad Lewis—and about 15 of his relatives and friends.

Oops.

"They were saying, 'Hey, what are you guys doing here?'" said Hale.

"But somehow," he continued, "that remained quiet. [Reid's name] didn't get out until later that year."

\* \* \* \* \*

He came with the reputation of being a single-minded, almost obsessive coach. When he got to Provo, he did nothing to dispel the notion.

Crowton wasn't one to skip details. Consider the way he prepared for games. In a Provo *Daily Herald* article in August 2002, Dick Harmon detailed Crowton's security measures. Practices were closed to the public. Media members could only attend certain practices, and even then needed to be checked off via clipboard. Four student security guards from the school's guest services screened visitors; two watched the only gate into practice, two others watched the perimeter.

There were even hand-held walkie-talkie radio sets for eight or so staffers who watched the sidelines for spies.

According to Harmon, Crowton was shocked in 2002 when he opened his first scrimmage to find a crowd of nearly 4,000. Getting close with the fans is one thing, but leaving yourself open to subterfuge is another.

An additional problem: the internet. The story reported that technology is a two-edged sword. Crowton assigned an administrative assistant to check message boards, chat rooms, team sites and newspapers for any scraps of information that might be helpful.

At the same time, such preparation can work both ways. In 1998, LaVell Edwards learned how important—or dangerous— the internet could be when he received a play-by-play account of a University of Washington scrimmage from a fan, via e-mail.

The next week, Edwards began closing practices.

\* \* \* \* \*

Edwards always commanded the respect of his players. Yet he was a low-key sort of coach. He wasn't big on rules and regulations and sometimes team meetings were fairly casual affairs.

Not so with Crowton.

Crowton's first words to his team won players over immediately. He met with them prior to the press conference in which he was introduced.

"Where's Doman?" he said.

Quarterback Brandon Doman, who had carried in the winning touchdown a few days earlier against Utah, raised his hand.

"I'm here," he said.

"Way to get in the end zone, Doman!" Crowton said.

The new coach proceeded to tell players to take their hats off, put their feet on the ground and "listen up."

"I want everyone to stand up. Then this half of the room to sit down."

When half the room sat down, he said, "All right. This is the percentage of football players who are graduating now. That is totally unacceptable. We're going to change that now. From here on, we will be students, and we are going to graduate."

The tone was set. Crowton wanted their attention. He wanted respectful behavior. And he wanted college *student* athletes.

Any questions?

He didn't think so.

\* \* \* \* \*

Crowton was noted as a great motivational speaker, particularly when talking to players at halftime.

"He's so good," said Hale, "he had me in tears for the Air Force game in 2001."

One trick he was known to do to motivate—and loosen—his team was to sing country songs. A favorite: The Charlie Daniels Band's "The Devil Went Down to Georgia."

After beating Wyoming in Laramie in 2001, Crowton began singing on the team bus, as it drove to Cheyenne, using the driver's microphone. Once Crowton was finished, he opened the mic up to anyone else on the bus. Karaoke night with the BYU Cougars.

One player after another got up. So did Hale, and even his wife. As one player, coach or administrator sat down, the remaining players would shout another name until he or she got up and sang.

"It was one of the most fun things we ever did," says Hale. "It was hilarious. I have never been more entertained."

And to think, *American Idol* wasn't there to capture it.

\* \* \* \* \*

Those who knew Crowton well say he admitted it—he was a lousy driver.

"He's always thinking of something else," said one athletic department staffer.

In the days right after Crowton was hired at BYU, he was driving a donor car from a local dealership, a Chevy Suburban. His mission was to scout out potential homes. After looking at one he liked, he began backing out of the driveway. *Crunch.* He had backed into the residence's brick mailbox.

Brand new car, new house and already he was beating them both up.

On the bright side, nobody could say he didn't have his mind on football.

\* \* \* \* \*

Smart guy. Friendly guy. But, boy, did Crowton think a lot about football. He spoke politely, yet always gave the impression he was thinking of something else—which he was.

Need evidence? Check with BYU traffic enforcement.

"Gary's first three cars—the Suburban, the black Audi and the gold Audi—he got in fender-benders with all three of them," said one football staffer.

All three were donor cars.

And all three were undoubtedly the result of his mind being on a play he wanted to try in a practice or game. Isn't there some sort of law? *No driver shall be allowed to devise football plays while operating a motor vehicle.*

The first accident was while he was looking at his new home. The other two were when he rear-ended other drivers as he talked football on the cell phone.

He even went to driving school—a requirement for any employee who gets in an accident on the BYU campus—and recorded perfect scores.

But if it's football season, campus traffic control beware.

# Chapter 5

## *The Quarterbacks*

Of all the quarterbacks that attended BYU, none was better under pressure than Jim McMahon. His 41-yard touchdown pass to Clay Brown on the last play of the 1980 Holiday Bowl is the most famous pass in school history.

What Garth Hall, a former running backs coach, remembers most about that night in San Diego was McMahon's calm as the coaches rushed about madly. With three seconds left on the clock, the Cougars called time out to discuss the play.

"All the coaches were running around, everyone was going back and forth on what to do. I looked over and saw McMahon, with his helmet cocked up on his head, getting a drink," said Hall.

Hall said as the coaching staff scrambled to set up the final play, McMahon looked at the heated exchanges going on, and finally said, "Oh, hell, I'll call it."

"Then he walks away and comes out to the huddle. The [players'] version is that he told them to run a 60-max protection, which has both backs stay back and block. But he just said to 'run like hell and I'll throw it up.' That's how he called it," said Hall.

And they say football is a complicated game.

\* \* \* \* \*

Each of the All-American quarterbacks had great qualities. One of McMahon's greatest was making teammates believe.

"He was always on the edge," continued Hall, "always kind of testing it. That swagger of his affected the whole club. To him, it was no big deal back then to go and play at Wisconsin."

It was that attitude that paved the way for one of BYU's greatest seasons, too.

In 1980 the Cougars won 34-7 at Hawaii. Beating the Rainbow Warriors that year wasn't so much a surprise as some of the methods they used.

That year the Cougars had struggled at times with their punting game. Clay Brown, the tight end, was also a powerful kicker, but his placement wasn't particularly good. As the coaching staff debated on what to do, it came up with an alternative plan—use McMahon for the times when accuracy was paramount.

Most fans forget McMahon was a respectable punter. "He could make plays," said former assistant coach Dick Felt. "He was extremely confident."

With his leg, as well as his arm.

There was some doubt McMahon would even play against Hawaii. A shoulder injury the previous Saturday had him on the sidelines all week.

"He does have, and is going to have, a problem with his arm," Edwards said in the week preceding the game. "I just hope it isn't too serious, but he didn't have much zip on the ball and hasn't practiced all week."

But start he did, throwing a phenomenal 60 passes.

The play of the game, though, wasn't on a pass. It came on a second-quarter situation in which McMahon took the snap on fourth and six, with the game tied. McMahon had to leap and raise his left arm just to tip the ball back into his grasp when snapped. As a defensive lineman swarmed in, McMahon stepped aside, allowing the opponent to fly past. Rushing to his left under pressure, he booted the ball on the run—with his left foot—33 yards.

The ball rolled out of bounds on the Hawaii one-yard line.

Small wonder McMahon had swagger. And even smaller wonder the Cougars had such confidence in him.

\* \* \* \* \*

Despite his competitive persona, McMahon could also be a gentleman. True, he liked drinking, swearing and thumbing his nose at the administration. But he was also kind to those he respected.

Hall invited the backfield and receivers to his home for Thanksgiving one year. His wife cooked several turkeys, "which they devoured in 10 minutes." There were also 50 pounds of potatoes and a dozen pumpkin pies.

After the dinner, Hall told the players they could retire to the TV room to eat pie and watch a football game. Each of the players headed immediately for the basement, except McMahon.

He unassumingly asked Hall's wife if he could help with the dishes. Then he stayed until the final dish was done.

"That's Jim," said Hall. "He's a dichotomy. He's a good father, good husband…that's the other part of him."

* * * * *

Regardless of the fact that McMahon wasn't a straight-laced Mormon—in fact, he wasn't a Mormon at all—he was widely respected by teammates and coaches.

"A born leader," said Hall.

"I remember once [offensive coordinator] Doug Scovil called him over after one play and said, 'You didn't read that play right; you threw it into double coverage,'" Hall recalled. "Jim said, 'I know, but I knew I could get the ball there.'"

Continued Hall, "He didn't care what the reads were, if he decided he wanted to throw, he knew he could get it there. He didn't have a real strong arm, but he could put the ball where his guys could get it.

"He was one of those guys with a presence; he had that feel for the field. He had so much confidence and accuracy. If he had to throw it hard, he could. He was almost at half-speed in practice, but if he had to zip it, he'd get it done."

Though each of BYU's quarterbacks had remarkable talents, McMahon had the most attitude. Hall said, for example, Marc Wilson was a quiet leader whom teammates respected and wanted to please. Gifford Nielsen was charismatic, directing everything, a big star as a student, leader and athlete from his junior high school days through college. Steve Young was versatile and gritty and could surprise even teammates with his freelancing.

"But Jim had that swagger," Hall continued. "He brought everyone to a higher elevation."

\* \* \* \* \*

McMahon never made it a secret that he didn't like BYU as an institution. But even after leaving school, he was adamant in his respect for LaVell Edwards.

Part of the reason was that Edwards had an ability to relate to non-LDS players in his program.

Some of McMahon's conflicts with BYU were of his own making. For instance, the times he would covertly lift mini-bottles from the airline serving carts and pour them into his Coke. Other times, though, he was completely innocent. At BYU, where violation of the honor code is a major infraction, McMahon was a constant target.

Those who either wanted him punished or merely thought they saw him in violation sometimes singled out McMahon.

"[My dad] would get calls from people saying, 'I saw him doing this or I saw him doing that,' when my dad was with him all the time," said Edwards's daughter, Ann Cannon.

Sometimes it was merely well-meaning people, she said, though occasionally it became "a tyranny of the crackpots."

Jimmy Mac couldn't have agreed more.

\* \* \* \* \*

There was Good Jim.

Then there was Bad Jim. Or at least Crazy Jim.

One season, the Cougars were in Hawaii for a game against the Rainbow Warriors, but that wasn't the only thing that was on wide receiver Dan Plater's mind.

The other was an upcoming exam.

Sequestered in his hotel room on the 26th floor of the Princess Kaiulaini hotel on Waikiki Beach, he was poring over his textbooks. His balcony door was open as the ocean breeze blew in.

The Cougars had come several days ahead of the game in

order to acclimate themselves against jet lag. As Plater worked, he heard scraping and scuffling above his room.

"All of a sudden," said Plater, "I see this pair of legs hanging down from the balcony above me. Then I see him swing out so he could get enough momentum to land on my balcony. When he lands, I look and it's Jim!

"He just comes walking in, no big deal. I said, 'What are you doing?' All he said was, 'Hey, what's up? How you doin'?'"

Fine, no doubt.

But couldn't he just have knocked?

\* \* \* \* \*

On the other end of the quarterback spectrum was Gifford Nielsen, a Provo-born local hero who seemed to do everything right.

Nielsen was, according to Ann Cannon, "this golden boy."

"Even in junior high and high school, he was very slick and polished. If he ever ran for an office, he got it. So, frankly, I wasn't inclined to like him very much.

"But when he got to college, he was one of Dad's favorites. He was really tough, hard-working and he wouldn't quit. Dad really liked Gifford."

Considering the fact that everything went well for Nielsen, he could have been a first-class jerk when he got to BYU.

"He could have been someone I ended up not liking, but he turned out to be the real thing," said Ann.

Golden is as golden does.

\* \* \* \* \*

Shortly after Steve Young signed his professional contract for a reported $40 million with the Los Angeles Express, he demonstrated just how young he still was.

He was returning to BYU from a trip regarding his new contract, and Edwards was unable to pick Young up at the Salt Lake City airport. So he asked his daughter, who was then married, to pick him up and take him to her home, not far away. Edwards

*Gifford Nielsen was a natural leader who always won whatever he tried out for. (Photo by Mark Philbrick, BYU Photo)*

would drive up from Provo to retrieve his former star.

"I got him in the car," said Ann, "and all the way home, he was talking about a test he had coming up, saying, 'I just know that history professor is going to give us a pop quiz.' He was obsessing and worrying over a pop quiz. I wanted to say, 'Pal, forget the pop quiz. You're worth $40 million.'"

The experience also gave Ann a perspective that wealth doesn't necessarily mean sophistication.

"It was an interesting insight," she said, "because all of a sudden he seemed pretty young. You see guys on TV—he looked like an Adonis, larger than life—and I pick him up at the airport and he's just a kid. He looked so young, in that respect. Young and nervous."

\* \* \* \* \*

Steve Young was the most successful of all the BYU quarterbacks once he got to the pros. But he was one of the least likely when he first came to the school.

Originally projected as a defensive back, he was determined to become the next great Cougar quarterback. So on the first down of his first practice in a BYU uniform, he did what any self-respecting quarterback would do—he fell on his seat.

The players were working out in shorts in the August heat. Young stepped behind the center, took the snap, stepped back three paces, and dropped flat.

It is said the journey of a thousand miles begins with one step.

Who knew that in Young's case, the first step would be backward?

\* \* \* \* \*

In 1980, Young was a lowly scrub playing on the junior varsity team.

But even then he had his good points. One of them was that he had been an option quarterback in high school.

That year, Wyoming was running an option offense. So the Cougar coaching staff drafted Young off the JV team to run that

*Steve Young was an "Adonis"—but still a kid in real life.*
*(Photo by Mark Philbrick, BYU Photo)*

offense against the first team defense in practice.

He ran it so well that the Cougars romped to a 52-17 home-coming win over the Cowboys.

The next week, Young was scheduled to start for the JV team in a game against UNLV. Naturally, the Rebels planned all week to face a typical pass-happy Cougar offense.

But Young had run the option so well in practice that the coaches decided to see what would happen if the junior varsity team ran the option against UNLV. They ran it, completely catching the Rebel team off guard.

It ended up a BYU rout, the same as usual.

The only difference was that that time they did it on the ground.

\* \* \* \* \*

Any coach or player who worked with one of BYU's great quarterbacks will tell you the same thing: each was a leader, but each had his own distinctive style.

Jim Edwards, son of LaVell, was a BYU receiver in 1981. He then served an LDS mission at the time when the church was sending male missionaries for 18 months. He returned to redshirt in 1983, then played the 1984, 1985 and 1986 seasons.

In the process, he got a wide variety of experiences, playing with Jim McMahon, Steve Young, Robbie Bosco and Steve Lindsley.

"With Jim McMahon," said the younger Edwards, "there was just never any question in anybody's mind that he was going to be the leader, in charge of the huddle. He was going to do it. Steve [Young] had that same command. They all had that presence in the huddle, though they all had different personalities."

Young was such a gifted athlete that he "made an added weapon" with his ability to run. Bosco wasn't nearly so fast, but "one thing he could do was throw the ball on time, and he was pretty darn accurate with it."

Continued Jim Edwards, "This might be prejudiced, because we were freshmen together, but Robbie so totally played within the system that it became so effective. Even after he was injured in our senior year—he had that bad arm—he got the ball up and on time, which is important, because a lot of interceptions are caused when the quarterback sits and waits too long."

Bosco came to BYU under enormous pressure. Not only had his predecessors been great, but also he had committed after the Cougars had failed to sign the highly touted Sean Salisbury, who chose USC instead.

"Robbie kind of had a chip on his shoulder, in that he needed to prove that he was as good as Salisbury or better than [teammate] Blaine Fowler, who was an awfully gifted quarterback, as well," said Jim Edwards.

He added, "He just played in the system maybe better than any of the quarterbacks. He just had total confidence and was never afraid to make the play within the system."

A lesser-known quarterback was Lindsley, who led the Cougars in 1986, following Bosco.

Jim Edwards pointed out that Lindsley never reached the stature of his more famous predecessors, but there were some good reasons. Among them was that they lost several fine receivers to graduation. "He didn't have the same opportunities to succeed as some of the others, so it didn't work out as well," he said.

Lindsley did fine anyway. He ended up as a broadcasting executive in Salt Lake City.

Once a leader, always a leader—whether you're an All-American or not.

\* \* \* \* \*

Bosco's first start at BYU couldn't have been more intimidating.

The Cougars were playing at Pittsburgh. The Panthers were rated No. 3 nationally, going into the first game of the 1984 season. The game was also among the first national TV games televised live by ESPN.

So there it was—a new quarterback, a national audience, and a nationally ranked opponent.

"I remember warming up and seeing the [Goodyear] blimp," said Bosco. "Everyone was nervous, but I was also nervous about what the past BYU quarterbacks had done. I didn't want to be the first who wasn't successful."

The first offensive play for BYU called for Mark Bellini to run a five-yard hitch route. He did so. Unfortunately, Bosco threw a pass that sailed far above Bellini's head.

"The ball came out of my hand like a curveball," said Bosco. "It rotated the opposite way it was supposed to. It had this sort of upward spiral like a helicopter. Mark didn't even jump for it. I'm like, 'It was my fault. I'll be OK on the next play.'"

Or not.

On the next play, Adam Haysbert was supposed to run a "speed-out" pattern. But on the way, he "makes a little move," and Bosco's throw hit him in the back of the helmet.

"I'm like, 'Goodness, I'm horrible,'" Bosco remembered.

The third pass was also incomplete.

Bosco was 0 for 1984.

"Not only was I 0 for three," said Bosco, "I wasn't even close. I'm walking to the sidelines, wondering if I should be out there. I was having trouble calming down, my heart was pounding. It was quite the entrance."

Bosco said that was the only time he ever considered dropping out.

"After that first series, I sincerely came off the field wondering if I was the guy to do this."

The next series, though, Bosco started completing passes. Gradually, he and teammates shook off the jitters. A handoff to Lakei Heimuli resulted in a touchdown and the Cougars were on the move.

"It was like, "Ahhh! We scored. We're gonna be OK," said Bosco.

And they were.

Interestingly, it was Coach Edwards who calmed Bosco down.

"It was one of the great moments of my career. LaVell met me a fourth of the way on the field. I'm thinking he might be coming out to tell me to sit down," recalled Bosco. "But he put his arm around me and said, 'Hey, relax. You're the guy. We know you can do it.' From that time on, he gave me a sense that people were behind me; I wasn't out there by myself. He just gave a great sense and feel that I could do things out there and that I would be OK."

\* \* \* \* \*

How tough was it to follow Virgil Carter, Gary Sheide, Gifford Nielsen, Marc Wilson, Jim McMahon and Steve Young?

When Bosco first arrived at BYU, the Cougars were coming off a year in which McMahon set numerous NCAA passing records. The next year Young was the quarterback. It wasn't as spectacular as the one McMahon had, but still good enough to win the WAC title. Young was easily an All-American. In 1983 the Cougars went 11-1, averaging nearly 600 yards a game in offense.

"I'm like, 'How in the world am I going to live up to this?' said Bosco. 'What is there that I can do that these guys haven't done? I'm not going to break 90 records. There's just nothing to go above it.'"

Actually, there was.

Win a national championship.

\* \* \* \* \*

Young was somewhat uncomfortable with his fame, at least in the early years.

When he left BYU to play in the USFL, he signed what at the time was the richest contract in pro football history. His younger brother, Mike, was on an LDS mission.

On his way home at the end of his mission, the younger Young got in a conversation with a football fan who noted Steve's enormous $40 million contract. Mike hadn't been told a word about it.

\* \* \* \* \*

Confidence was never a problem with any of the great quarterbacks. When Young was a sophomore, he was listed after the

*Robbie Bosco had the challenge of trying to live up to the quarterback legacy.*
*(Photo by Mark Philbrick, BYU Photo)*

first week of practice as the No. 4 quarterback.

"He was way upset," said Jim Edwards. "He couldn't believe it. By the time fall practice was over, he had moved to No. 2 behind McMahon. He thought he should be the starter. That's how he viewed himself and what he accepted. He was never going to accept being a defensive back; he knew he wanted to be quarterback at BYU. Even when he was second behind McMahon, he accepted being second grudgingly."

Trouble with overtaking McMahon was they both had the same attitude. When McMahon was a freshman, the team traveled to Japan to play an exhibition game at the end of the season. Gifford Nielsen had been hurt and was on crutches, and Marc Wilson had taken over the top spot, with McMahon as the backup.

That went over poorly with McMahon.

"I was in high school and went with the team to Japan," said Jim Edwards. "I still remember being in the hotel lobby and the guys were sitting around, and Jim [McMahon] said, 'I'll tell you right now, I'm better than either of those guys.'"

Added the younger Edwards, "He was serious. He wasn't joking. He had that kind of attitude about him."

As it turned out, he *was* better.

It's just that at the time, he was the only one who knew.

\* \* \* \* \*

As colorful and controversial as McMahon was, he was respected by teammates. That's because he treated them with respect.

Forget the guy who blew his nose on a reporter and mooned a TV helicopter when he was playing in the NFL.

Blaine Fowler, another former BYU quarterback, came to training camp a couple of weeks early as a freshman, and began working out with teammates. One drill involved having the quarterbacks in one line, parallel to a line of receivers. The receiver would run a route and catch the pass.

On his first trip to the front of the line, the inexperienced Fowler looked over to see veteran receiver Danny Plater looking across at him. Plater stepped back into the line and told a freshman receiver to catch Fowler's pass.

"I'm thinking, 'That was kind of rude,'" recalled Fowler.

Next time at the front of the line...same thing.

McMahon, who was actually a good friend of Plater's, said to Fowler, "Oh, don't mind him. He's an [expletive]. Don't worry about it."

The next round, McMahon came up across from Plater. But rather than taking his turn, McMahon turned to Fowler and said, "Hey, Blaine, you take this," thus putting Fowler alongside Plater again.

"To this day, whenever I see Jim McMahon, he has always been very, very kind to me," said Fowler. "He was always very gracious."

Besides, said Fowler, he helped him in other areas. When they were in Hawaii, staying in the Princess Kaiulaini, the rooms looked down over the International Marketplace. There was a considerable updraft, which would blow up past the balconies of the player rooms.

McMahon taught Fowler and others to take a roll of toilet paper and hold the end, then let it unravel. The updraft would make the tissue paper sail high above the hotel.

"All the quarterbacks were great guys," recalled kicker Kurt Gunther, who played with McMahon, Wilson, and Young and saw Bosco enter the program.

"But Jim was, I would say, the most fun and most motivational guy to play with. He's the kind of guy that if someone screwed up, he would be the first to come up and smack you on the butt and tell you that you're the best. He would say something like, 'You'll probably have to kick the winning field goal, so get your act together. You're the best.' Players would do anything for him.

"I really believe the only guy who felt we could win that [1980] Holiday Bowl was Jim. He felt it every second, that 'we're going to win; we can win this game!' It takes a special kind of athlete to instill that kind of motivation and confidence."

\* \* \* \* \*

Nobody ever said Bosco couldn't take pain.

Not then, not now.

Bosco, who limped his way to victory in the 1984 Holiday Bowl—securing a national title—played most of his senior season with an injured shoulder. He never quite shook his penchant for injuries.

Even in the summer of 2000, long after going into coaching, injuries seemed to follow him. He was working in his yard one day and stuck his hand in some weeds. He felt a sting, but thought nothing of it.

Until his arm began to ache.

Next thing he knew, he was in the emergency room. The lymph nodes in his arms began throbbing and his arm went numb. Soon his legs felt the same. At Utah Valley Regional Medical Center, he was told he had been bitten by a black widow. He was given medication for the pain, treated and hospitalized.

Next summer, Bosco again ended up in the emergency room. That time he was in Park City riding a bike, when it crashed. The result: a separated shoulder.

There's more.

In July of 2002, he was jogging on a pathway near the mouth of Provo Canyon, when he was hit by a teenaged bicyclist. "He came around a corner and I got hit head-on," Bosco told the *Deseret News.*

He suffered a deep thigh bruise, but wasn't hospitalized.

What is the reason for the rash of non-football injuries? Bosco has no clue.

But he does admit it has been weird.

"It's been pretty crazy the last couple of years," he told the *News.*

\* \* \* \* \*

Quarterbacks are admired for their leadership skills. But an oft-overlooked skill is the ability to listen. In at least one case, it helped win the Heisman trophy.

For years the BYU training staff has required its quarterbacks to wear a brace on the left knee, if it was a right-handed quarterback. That's because the leg is highly vulnerable. Too often quarterbacks are hit by a charging opponent—or even their own offensive linemen stumbling backward—and injured.

When Ty Detmer arrived at BYU, trainer George Curtis handed Detmer a brace and told him to wear it in all games. Detmer complied.

A couple of weeks later, Detmer approached Curtis.

"Mr. Curtis," he said in his soft South Texas drawl. "Do you mind if I ask you a question? Why do all the quarterbacks have to wear a knee brace?"

Curtis explained to him the vulnerability of the left leg.

"OK," said Detmer.

Some quarterbacks have hated the brace and balked at wearing one. Not Detmer. Never in his time at the school did he need to be reminded to wear his brace.

Brandon Doman, the Cougars' 2001 starting quarterback, actually talked the coaches out of making him wear one. But he had a good case. He argued, successfully, that he wasn't planting in the pocket. As an option quarterback, he was more often sprinting to the outside.

Others learned by experience. John Walsh, BYU's starting quarterback in 1993 and 1994, had three braces torn off or mangled in a single game. Once, when the Cougars pulled him out of the game, he thought his knee had locked. Instead, it was a damaged brace that wouldn't allow him to extend. It had been twisted so badly that the training staff had to cut the brace off.

Usually the quarterbacks argued about the brace. Curtis could only tell them what any parent tells his kid: "I'm doing it for your own good."

\* \* \* \* \*

A common thread among all BYU's great quarterbacks was their competitiveness—in everything. Ever want to turn lunch into a competitive event? Enlist a quarterback.

After leaving college, Steve Young moved on to play for the Los Angeles Express of the old United States Football League.

George Curtis, then the trainer for the Express, golfed with Young regularly.

One year they were playing at a course in Anaheim, California, that had a dogleg left. Young hit the ball and it faded into a dry riverbed. Young disappeared below the bank, vowing not to lose the ball. He stuck his head up and called to Curtis: "Here comes the ball!"

Young disappeared again and a moment later the ball came flying nicely out of the riverbed and onto the green. He two-putted for par.

"What's your score [on that hole]?" said Curtis.

"Four," Young deadpanned.

"Four? How'd you get a four? You hit it into the river!"

Young patiently explained that the first shot went in the river, the second one came out, then the two-putt.

Four.

"So," said Curtis. "How come you hit a yellow ball in and an orange one came out?"

\* \* \* \* \*

Ty Detmer was a practical joker. But he also wasn't above a little misdirection when it came to dealing with the coaches.

One of his favorite tricks was placing the blame on someone other than himself. In the BYU system, plays were sent in via receivers. Sometimes he would change the play in the huddle. If all went well, the coaches never said anything. If it didn't work, they would ask Detmer why he didn't run their play.

Invariably, he would say in serious tones that he ran the play the receiver brought in. That way the coaches wouldn't blame him. Either the receiver got blamed, or the coaches assume something got crossed in the translation.

\* \* \* \* \*

The first day Detmer showed up for practice in 1988, there was a buzz of excitement that went through the team. The players had all heard about the heralded quarterback from Texas who had smashed so many records.

But when he showed up, they were stunned.

"We were expecting a six-four, 220-pound guy," said Chuck Cutler, who was a wide receiver at BYU. "Out walks this six-foot, 150-pound kid. We're like, 'You gotta be kidding me. This is what we've been hearing about? This is the best we can do?' Initially, that's how we felt about it."

It didn't take Detmer long, however, to establish credibility. Cutler recalls running a curl pattern against Utah during his senior year. The pass was complete, but he had rounded the curl, rather than coming straight back.

Detmer was just a freshman, but when the play was over, he went straight for Cutler, who was a senior and a team captain.

"He let me know right then that I was curling my patterns and I needed to come straight back. He was right, too," said Cutler. "I knew then he would be good."

\* \* \* \* \*

One thing that made Detmer great was the joy he incorporated into his game. For him, it wasn't all that different than a Saturday morning sandlot outing.

"With Detmer, it was as if we were playing in the back yard," said Cutler. "He would change plays. He used to say, 'Hey, Chuck, run it a little deeper this time,' or 'Try this, this time.' That's what made him fun. He was fun to play with, he enjoyed the game and it was just like in the back yard—'go down the corner and around the garage and come on out.' It's what made him a great one."

\* \* \* \* \*

In Detmer's senior year, BYU traveled to Miami, where it absorbed a 41-17 defeat.

Detmer didn't take the defeat easily.

On one play he got drilled as he was going out of bounds and was flopping around on the sidelines, trying to get up. One of the officials came over to help Detmer to his feet.

"Why didn't you throw a flag, you [expletive]?" Detmer screamed, hoping the umpire would penalize Miami for a late hit.

So the official complied. He did throw a flag—on Detmer. Unsportsmanlike conduct.

After the penalty, one of his fellow officials said, "What did he say to you?"

The official, unaware his microphone was still live, said, "He called me a [expletive]!"

The entire stadium heard the exchange and responded with laughter.

\* \* \* \* \*

Detmer's practical joke side was always there—even when it involved injuries.

After the 1987 and 1988 seasons, Cutler had surgeries on his hands. While recovering the second time, they were put in a cast-like contraption that had rubber bands attached to each finger and stretched to the fingertips. The idea was to force him to exercise his hands regularly.

It was a rather complicated-looking piece of medical machinery.

But Detmer thought it was funny. One day at an off-season meeting, Cutler came in wearing the familiar hand brace. A moment later Detmer arrived. He was wearing a contraption he had made on his own to look like Cutler's. Only Detmer made his with cardboard, rubber bands and paper clips.

"If Chuck's gonna wear one," said Detmer, "we're all gonna wear 'em."

\* \* \* \* \*

Once upon a time, the Cougars held a team luau during training camp. The idea was a combination of two things: to promote team unity and honor the significant number of Pacific Islanders playing on the team.

*Ty Detmer was good for more than a few laughs—and touchdowns.*
*(Photo by Mark Philbrick, BYU Photo)*

And it's not a great luau unless there is a roasted pig.

Through means and methodology that have grown hazy with time, Detmer procured the head of the pig. After the luau, he took it home to his dorm room, which he shared with teammate Mike O'Brien. He then placed the pig's head, a la *The Godfather*, in O'Brien's bed.

Said former team video coordinator Chad Bunn, "Mike wouldn't sleep in his bed for a month."

\* \* \* \* \*

It must have been something about animals in the apartment.

Pig head wasn't the only thing that ended up in Detmer's living quarters.

Sometime in his career, Detmer picked up the habit of going to nearby East Bay golf course and fishing in one of the ponds. He would catch several carp, bring them home, and put them in the tub.

Roommates would come home late at night, go to bed, and the next morning half-asleep, step into the shower, only to recoil in horror at the sight of several carp swimming in their tub.

\* \* \* \* \*

Bunn had another recollection of Detmer's playful side.

The 1988 Cougars played in Anaheim at the Freedom Bowl. Bunn, who accompanied the team, was with his wife, eating at an Arby's restaurant on Harbor Boulevard one afternoon.

Plop!

Plop! Plop!

The sound was coming from the windows, right next to where Bunn and his wife were eating.

Plop!

Bunn looked out toward the street. There, taking shots from the sidewalk with a paintball gun was Detmer, who had seen his BYU friend and decided to open fire.

So passing wasn't the only thing he did with pinpoint accuracy.

\* \* \* \* \*

Sean Covey was in a tough spot. He followed a long line of not just good, but national-class quarterbacks. He carried the weight of the tradition on his shoulders. Truth is, his talents would have been fine at almost any other school.

But they were below expectations at BYU.

Former teammate Cutler said the difference between Detmer and Covey was that Detmer was having fun. Covey had been heard to say he stopped having fun playing football when he got to college.

Sometimes the drive to succeed was, well, obsessive. For example, there was the year the Cougars were awaiting a game in Provo. They had gathered in the locker room to dress for kickoff. Covey abruptly arose and hustled out the door.

Teammates stared, trying to figure out what was going on. "What happened to Sean?" they asked one another.

A few minutes later, Covey returned and began getting dressed in his uniform.

According to Cutler, when someone asked where he had been, Covey replied, "I drove to the stadium the wrong way."

He was superstitious enough that he realized he had taken an alternate route to the stadium. To right the wrong, he drove back home and returned via his normal route.

\* \* \* \* \*

Covey wasn't the only superstitious quarterback.

In 1995-96, junior college transfer Steve Sarkisian, now coach of the Washington Huskies, ran the Cougar offense. He had a phenomenal year in 1996, leading the Cougars to a 14-1 record and a Cotton Bowl victory.

His routine didn't include driving the same route to the stadium. His involved the goal posts. He would walk the length of the field and around each of the goal posts, touching them as he circled. More than superstition, it may have been a case of

*Ty Detmer won the Heisman at BYU in 1990.*
*(Photo by Mark Philbrick, BYU Photo)*

practicing a routine that relaxed him.

"I understand he had done that for years," said Duane Busby, the team's football operations director. "But I can never remember a situation, even in bad weather, when he didn't do that."

\* \* \* \* \*

During the 1985 game at Temple, a fight erupted. Glen Kozlowski, the pro-bound receiver for BYU, ended up in a scuffle in one of the end zones, right in front of a group of rowdy fans.

The scuffle began when teammate Jeff Sprowls and a Temple player began shoving one another. Soon Kozlowski was overdefending him. As things escalated, both benches emptied and headed for the end zone.

Except for a couple of the quarterbacks, that is.

"I'm sitting on the bench," said Blaine Fowler, and "Robbie [Bosco] is sitting next to me. We have our Gatorade in our hands, and all of a sudden, everyone leaves to go down to the end zone. We're feeling sort of naked. Robbie and I are on the bench and every other player and coach is in the end zone. I'm feeling a little embarrassed."

After watching the proceedings from a distance, Fowler looked at Bosco and said, "Rob, should we be involved?"

The laid-back Bosco wasn't about to take the bait.

"Hey," said Bosco, with a dismissive grin. "We're quarterbacks, man."

\* \* \* \* \*

The Cougars won the 1988 Freedom Bowl, 20-17 over Colorado, largely due to two fourth-quarter field goals.

And despite Detmer's misgivings.

Urging his teammates on during the final scoring drive, Detmer told his offensive teammates: "We've gotta get the ball in the end zone. You just can't trust those kickers to get it done for you!"

As it turned out, two field goals by Jason Chaffetz—now a U.S. Representative—provided the tying and winning points.

* * * * *

For some time during the 1988 season, the Cougars had searched to find a permanent quarterback. Covey was off and on. At varying times, athletic department officials and coaches had urged Edwards to try the young Detmer.

But Edwards resisted. He liked his quarterbacks to have more seasoning. He preferred remaining loyal to the upperclassmen.

It was the Freedom Bowl that year that changed everything, though. Trailing 14-7 at halftime, things didn't look especially good for the Cougars.

"We kept telling LaVell to give Detmer a shot," said Pete Witbeck, a retired athletic department official, who died in 2010. No go.

Finally, though, Covey went down with an injury. Now Edwards's hand was forced. He had to play Detmer.

The rest is history. Detmer led the Cougars to a comeback win over Colorado.

As Witbeck was walking off the field with Edwards, the long-time coach said, "Pete, I think I've found myself a quarterback."

* * * * *

His career was short and uneventful. Bret Engemann came to BYU a highly regarded quarterback. But after losing his starting job during the 2002 season, he announced he would leave school and enter the NFL draft.

The media liked Engemann. He was articulate, accommodating and always showed up for interviews. But his relationship with teammates could be a bit more complicated. Like, for instance, the day in the spring of 2003 when former teammate C. J. Ah You cold-cocked him, just before Engemann worked out for pro scouts. Reports said Ah You thought Engemann was flirting with his girlfriend.

When Engemann began at BYU, there was a tradition of upperclassmen shaving the heads of freshmen. They accomplished the task each year on the night before two-a-days started.

"Usually," recalled former defensive lineman Hans Olsen, "there was no fuss."

That was before Engemann arrived.

When players surrounded Engemann to shave his head, he let them know he wasn't going to cooperate. There were threats, shouts and, according to Olsen, "things went to blows. He started hitting [teammate] Dustin Rykert, starts throwing a fit."

Eventually the players backed off. Still angry about the incident, Engemann "ended up telling LaVell," who wasn't amused.

"That was the end of the head-shaving," said Olsen. "We haven't shaved anyone's head after that incident."

\* \* \* \* \*

Most of the time a quarterback makes it a point to get along with his offensive line. Otherwise, it could mean disaster. But once in a while, he has to call a meeting to order.

That was the case on September 15, 1984.

Offensive lineman Trevor Matich was out with an injury, so guard Robert Anae moved over to center. That week the Cougars were playing Tulsa. Though Tulsa wasn't an overly dangerous team, it did have an imposing nose guard.

"He was huge. He was about six foot nine—the biggest nose guard I had ever seen," said Bosco. "When he would get down in his stance, I could almost see him eye to eye."

To further complicate matters, Anae was playing a new position, having moved from guard to center.

On the first play of the game, Bosco dropped back to pass. Well, almost.

"I don't take a step," Bosco said, "before [the nose guard] goes around Robert and throws me down."

Bosco caught Anae after the play and said, "Robert, you've got to be kidding me. You've got to be able to block this guy a little bit or we'll never get a play off!"

Bosco said he was mad at his center at the time. But to Anae's credit, "the guy never touched me the rest of the game."

# Chapter 6

## *Characters*

Todd Christensen, the BYU fullback who went on to a notable career in the NFL as a tight end, was easily challenged. All anyone had to do was tell him he couldn't do something. (Christensen even chose BYU over other schools because it was willing to let him play fullback, rather than linebacker.)

In Christensen's senior year (1977), the Cougars were practicing for the third game. BYU had struggled with its kicking execution, though the Cougars had remained undefeated. But concerns over the lack of steady long snapping had the coaches worried.

Garth Hall, an assistant coach, arrived at practice one day to see Christensen zipping snap after snap. Each was a perfect spiral.

"Todd," the coach said, "how come you didn't tell us you could snap?"

Said Christensen: "Nobody asked me."

Thereafter, they used Christensen for long snapping, and the team went on to a 9-2 season and tied for first place in the Western Athletic Conference.

Christensen continued into the pros, where he bounced around for awhile as a running back. After switching to tight end, he went on to play in two Super Bowls with the Raiders. The first one, he played as a running back (1981), but he was a starter in Super Bowl XVIII (1984) at tight end.

Who knew he could be such a good pro player?

Nobody asked.

\* \* \* \* \*

As with all good players, Christensen was highly competitive. During one practice while he was at BYU, the team was doing two-man sled blocking drills. Hall, who coached running backs, said, "I'll buy a steak dinner for anyone who can break this sled."

Enough said. Christensen was all over it.

As the practice progressed, players began slamming harder and harder against the sled; soon a crack appeared. By then the players were vigorously trying to break it apart. An air horn blew, just as the crack began to widen, signaling the next segment of practice was to begin. But Christensen gave it one more try, breaking the sled apart.

"Where's my steak?" he told Hall.

"You didn't break it before the horn blew," said Hall.

Remembered Hall: "I never did buy him one, but he was ready to kill me. I guess I'll have to buy him one someday. If you put a red flag up in front of him he could do anything."

Added Hall: "I think the bigger the challenge, the more Todd loved it. To tell him he couldn't do something is what drove him. It's what still drives him."

\* \* \* \* \*

Joe Scanlan was a BYU middle guard in 1966-67. A Hawaii native, he was big. He was strong. A man ahead of his time, he even mastered the art of referring to himself in third person.

One year the Cougars were getting off the bus at Wyoming to play a game. Scanlan walked inside a building and straight through a plate glass window. Glass shattered about him. Afterward, the silence was deafening.

Scanlan was unfazed.

"That's the cleanest window Big Joe's ever seen," he said dryly.

\* \* \* \* \*

According to BYU football legend, Scanlan and a teammate were crossing the street on another occasion to attend practice, just as a car pulled up to the stoplight. But it stopped too close for Scanlan's liking.

He picked up a large rock and began smashing the car.

Said Scanlan: "I'll show how Big Joe trains cars."

* * * * *

Hans Olsen was the nephew of NFL great Merlin Olsen. And like his famous uncle, Hans played the defensive line.

The elder Olsen was the more renowned player, going on to a Hall of Fame football career. His nephew, though, didn't do badly for himself. He made it in the NFL, playing for the Indianapolis Colts.

And he was clearly the superior humorist.

Reporters flocked to get near Olsen after games (and during the week, for that matter). First, he had that connection to his uncle. But second, he was hilarious. He appeared in *ESPN The Magazine*, balancing a couch on his chin as part of a story entitled "Freak Show." It featured college athletes with unusual hobbies.

It didn't really matter what subject Olsen was addressing. He was equally adept, whether expounding on pop culture, rock-and-roll, food or rushing a passer.

In August 2000, the Cougars played a game at Jacksonville against Florida State. It was a notable event, considering the Cougars were meeting the defending national champions. But there was another intriguing angle: They were playing against a team with someone older than they were.

For a team filled with married players and returned LDS missionaries, finding someone older was highly unusual. For instance, that year BYU had 25-year-old Tevita Ofahengaue, who was married with four children. Tyson Smith was nearly 25 when the game with FSU was played.

But the oldest player on the field was 28-year-old FSU quarterback Chris Weinke.

Ofahengaue good-naturedly noted the Cougars were just kids compared to Weinke. "At least I'm not the oldest now. They're not calling me grandpa any more," he said.

The best line, though, came from Olsen. Asked about Weinke's age, he mused, "Wonder what mission he went on."

\* \* \* \* \*

Olsen was also appreciated for his candor. That same season, as the BYU-Utah game approached, it lacked the usual buildup. The two teams' record going in was a combined 9-12.

Still, Olsen wasn't above remarking on the traditional rivalry anyway.

"Both teams could be 0-11 coming into that game, and it would still be big," he told the Salt Lake *Deseret News*. "The fact we've both had dumpy seasons, that's going to make it more of a battle, to see which team had the dumpier season. Hopefully we can end up and say they had the dumpier season."

Well said.

BYU ended up winning the game. Which meant that year Utah had the dumpier season.

\* \* \* \* \*

Olsen was a true character.

He knew it. The coaches knew it. *ESPN The Magazine* knew it.

For instance, there was the time the team was walking away from dinner the night before a game. Players had just filled up on barbecued chicken wings.

As they were leaving the dining area, Olsen spoke up.

"I think I'm in trouble," he said.

"Why's that?" said a teammate.

"Well," said Olsen, "I had 10 of those wings, but I only counted eight bones."

\* \* \* \* \*

Another highly quotable player was offensive lineman Jason Scukanec, who played with Olsen for part of his career.

Scukanec, a center, didn't often get noticed for his play. But his quotes were another story.

In the days leading up to the 2001 Liberty Bowl, the Cougars were short on running backs. Star player Luke Staley was out with an injury. Reno Mahe had converted to receiver. Ned Stearns and Paul Peterson had each broken a wrist. Senior Mike Nielsen, a little-used player, had been out all season, but was available. BYU even resorted to inserting safety Alex Farris into the offensive backfield for practice. He had played running back in high school.

But none of the above considerations suited Scukanec. He had his own brainstorm, and it involved fellow offensive lineman Isaac Herring.

Asked whom he thought should carry the ball in the bowl game, Scukanec didn't hesitate. "Isaac J. Herring," he told the *News*. "That's who they need to put in the backfield. No. 73. I'm calling out Coach Crowton right now. Why haven't they done it earlier? Why aren't they doing it right now? That solves the problem. Luke who? Isaac J. Herring. Five yards a carry, guaranteed. Won't find a better blocking back in the country. Weighs 330 pounds, and he runs a sub-five 40."

Suffice it to say Crowton wasn't listening, which was too bad.

Herring might have become the next Refrigerator Perry.

* * * * *

Nineteen-eighty was an eventful year, in which the Cougars won a conference championship and their first bowl game. But it was significant in another aspect, too. That was the season two Cougar players took their homework to a new level.

Receiver Dan Plater and cornerback Tom Holmoe were taking a vertebrate physiology course, with plans to eventually go to medical school. It was a tough course. The instructor wasn't about to cut any slack for a couple of football players who were heading to Hawaii.

The big game with the Rainbow Warriors was coming up, and a test was scheduled for the following Monday. But it wasn't a book test, it was a lab test. So Plater had an idea: Take their studies on the road.

Desperate times call for desperate measures.

The night before the team left for the Islands, Plater took

matters into his own hands. He walked into a classroom building, which was still open at that hour. To his good fortune, there was a connecting hallway between that and the building that housed the lab. Plater walked through undetected and found the door unlocked.

*Voila!*

He quickly grabbed a shark, a couple of turtles and a dove cadaver, and stuffed them into a football equipment bag, then stole off into the night. He was taking them with him on the trip.

All went well until they arrived at the Salt Lake airport the next day. Plater tried to put the bag through the security check as carry on luggage. The woman at the security screening saw the outline of animal bones on the monitor and exclaimed, "Oh my goodness!"

Assistant coach Tom Ramage heard the commotion and came over to investigate. When the bag was opened, there was a respectable sampling of the animal kingdom.

Said Ramage, "You never cease to amaze me, Plater."

The coaches thought it was a joke. Plater said it was homework.

When they landed in Hawaii, Plater and Holmoe took the cadavers to their room. The team had arrived a few days early, to acclimate for the Saturday game. Thus, Plater and Holmoe had time to spread the dead animals out on a table and conduct their studying. Afterward, they stuffed the remains in a dumpster.

"Amazing thing is," said Plater, "we aced the test."

Recalled Holmoe, "I'm sure Dan aced the test. I don't know about anyone else. But I know it was very beneficial to us. It's one thing to hear about guys bringing laptop computers on trips to study. We actually had to bring the lab with us."

\* \* \* \* \*

Ramage was right about one thing—Plater was amazing.

A likable and truly funny athlete, he considered it his sworn duty to keep things light in practice. One of his favorite targets was fellow receiver Lloyd Jones.

"I'd get him ticked off and get him kicked out of practice all the time," Plater said in hindsight.

Jones seemed to see conspiracy in a lot of things, particularly if he wasn't getting the plays called his way. Offensive coordinator Doug Scovil was constantly imploring Plater to leave Jones—who was known to lose his temper fairly easily—alone.

That season they were practicing for the Holiday Bowl, when Plater decided to open an old wound. The previous year, when the players were given their Holiday Bowl rings, their names had been on the outside of the boxes. Jones's was labeled "Floyd" Jones, rather than Lloyd. The mistake seriously annoyed Jones.

Plater said one day in practice, "Hey, Lloyd, remember last year when you got your Holiday Bowl ring with 'Floyd' on the box?"

"That was enough to get him going," Plater later recalled. "He threw a fit and eventually got kicked out of practice. LaVell was always saying, 'Why don't you leave the kid alone?'"

On another occasion, the team was practicing a play in which the ball was to be tossed to either Plater or Jones, and running back Scott Phillips would swing around on the hook-and-ladder play, take a pitch from the receiver and rush down the sidelines.

Trouble was, on that day Jones was apparently feeling neglected. Plater had been needling him again about the coaches not giving him enough opportunities. By the time Jones's turn came to practice the play, he was furious about the perceived slight.

The first time they ran the play, Jim McMahon tossed the ball to Jones near the sidelines. Just as Phillips was coming behind him for the pitch, Jones turned and ran 60 yards up field, never stopping, never looking back.

Offensive coordinator Doug Scovil said, "OK, that's fine. If someone is on Scott or if you're getting hit, go ahead and run it. But let's try to work on the timing. Let's pitch it next time."

Next play, same thing. McMahon stepped back, tossed to Jones, who charged 60 yards up field.

"Lloyd!" the coaches said. "What are you doing?"

Jones mumbled about getting short-changed on the play calling and wanting to run the ball. "This is bull!" he said. "I can

*Doug Scovil helped bring national attention to the Cougars' offensive attack.*
*(Photo by Mark Philbrick, BYU Photo)*

take it all the way every time."

The coaches explained that wasn't what they had in mind.

Meanwhile, Plater was whispering in Jones's ear: "You're getting cheated. You need to just carry it yourself!"

"Yeah," said Jones. "I know."

One more try.

McMahon dropped back. Jones caught the pass. Phillips headed over to take the pitch.

Jones ran straight down the field.

Recalled Plater, "They kick him out of practice. He walks off throwing his gear everywhere. By the time he gets to the end of the field, he's practically got his uniform off."

Edwards, who knew Plater's part in the incident, said, "Plater, sometimes I don't know whether to hug you or slug you."

For a period of time, the longtime BYU coach even banned Plater from the weight room. The receiver was so busy goading teammates into doing something foolish, Edwards decided the team would be better off with him somewhere else. He told him to "go play basketball or something."

"You mean," said an elated Plater, "I don't have to go lift weights and instead I get to play basketball?"

So *that's* what they mean when they say a "win-win" situation.

* * * * *

Jones could run a great pass route. It served him on more than one occasion.

A big track meet was going on one day at the Smith Field-house, when Jones came tearing into the building. Right behind him was a bunch of burly rugby players.

Jones had been on the practice field and become embroiled in a dispute. One thing led to another, and soon the ruggers were coming after Jones. Being a wide receiver, he was sure he could outrun them.

When they started after him, he raced into the fieldhouse to evade capture.

"He ran right through the track meet," recalled Gym Kimball, the former BYU reserve quarterback. "He ran a post pattern. We were all watching and recognized it. He was using his routes to get away from those guys."

Eventually security broke up the disturbance.

Before the rugby players broke up Jones.

\* \* \* \* \*

Occasionally someone got back at Plater.

But only occasionally.

One such occurrence was at a San Diego hotel as the Cougars prepared for the Holiday Bowl. Kickers Kurt Gunther and Lee Johnson had been sitting in the Jacuzzi and noticed a spot where air bubbles were coming out of the water. After some experimenting, they learned they could put their mouths down by an air portal and stay underwater for several minutes.

Not long after, Plater came out by the pool and sat down next to them.

"Hey," said Gunther, "let's make a bet on who can hold his breath the longest under water."

Plater was all in favor.

They all went down at the same time. But the two kickers made sure they were close to where the air was escaping.

Plater stayed under water for a minute or so, then came up gasping. The kickers remained.

Two minutes…three minutes…four….five.

Finally they popped up.

"I guess we won," said Gunther.

Unaware of the air portal they had been using, Plater didn't say a word. He got out of the Jacuzzi and grabbed his towel.

"That was disgusting," he said, and walked off into the night.

\* \* \* \* \*

Jim McMahon never did make himself out to be something he wasn't. And he wasn't one to keep his opinions to himself.

Late in the summer of 1980, prior to his junior season, Mc-

Mahon and teammates Ryan Tibbitts, Plater and Phillips went to a Provo golf course to play in a foursome.

The clubhouse was situated close enough to the first tee that patrons could watch golfers beginning their rounds. There was a large deck that overlooked the course.

On that day, a Cougar Club function was going on at the club. The place was packed with BYU fans. As the four Cougar players stepped to the tee, a considerable number of onlookers gathered on the deck.

The players could hear them whispering: "There's McMahon," "That's Plater," and "I think that's Scott Phillips."

McMahon stepped up to tee off. A good golfer, he nonetheless shanked his first shot into the trees along the fairway.

The crowd of BYU fans went suddenly silent. "You could have heard a pin drop," Tibbitts recalled.

The silence lasted a few seconds. McMahon grasped his driver, reared back and threw it 30 yards down the fairway, yelling an expletive.

So maybe he wasn't your model BYU student.

As McMahon marched angrily down the fairway, the crowd of onlookers whispered noisily about the demonstration.

Even though McMahon hadn't become a big star yet, this much they knew: The guy didn't like losing—at anything.

\* \* \* \* \*

As everyone who knew him could attest, McMahon had an edge.

Teammates loved him. Opponents respected him. The media clamored for him.

Cosmo the Cougar feared him.

The spring after the "Miracle Bowl" win over Southern Methodist, Plater, McMahon and Tibbitts decided to take in a BYU baseball game. McMahon had become a campus celebrity, thanks to his bowl-game heroics. He couldn't go anywhere in Provo without being asked about his game-winning throw.

By that spring, he had pretty much grown weary of recounting it.

One April day, the three players went over to Cougar Field and sat near the backstop. Hoping to not be recognized, McMahon had a ball cap pulled down and a pair of dark glasses. He just wanted to see the game.

Unfortunately, the team mascot spotted him in the stands. It's not like McMahon had a great disguise. He *always* wore sunglasses.

Cosmo came over to the trio and began pointing to McMahon, drawing the attention of the crowd. Then he began imitating a quarterback throwing a pass, striking poses and pointing again and again at McMahon.

McMahon ignored Cosmo for several minutes.

Cosmo continued. McMahon simmered. Finally, he had had enough. When Cosmo leaned over near McMahon's face, the quarterback grabbed him by the snout, pulled him close to his face and screamed, "[EXPLETIVE], COSMO!"

Cosmo retreated and McMahon settled back to watch the game.

Nobody bothered him the rest of the afternoon.

* * * * *

One of the most colorful players in BYU history never started a varsity game while there. In fact, he never even lettered. But he did have an impact.

The player was quarterback Gym Kimball.

That's right. G-Y-M.

He changed his name from Jim when he was in junior high, because he liked the connotation. "Back when I needed attention a lot more than I do now," he said.

A highly regarded quarterback from Salt Lake City, Kimball was stuck in a long succession of eight quarterbacks at BYU that included McMahon and Steve Young. Eventually he transferred to Utah State, where he became a starter.

Kimball was known for his offbeat sense of humor. During one team chalk-talk session at BYU, he was listening to offensive coordinator Doug Scovil talk about a series of plays.

In naming the plays, the quarterbacks and receivers were supposed to know from which slot the quarterback would pass. The play might be "Fake 38 Boot at 7." If he rolled out farther, it would be "Fake 38 Boot at 9."

That particular day, Scovil was going over the plays, when he called on Kimball to give him a sample play.

"OK," said Kimball, standing at the front of the meeting room. "Fake 38 Boot."

Scovil waited for Kimball to add the spot from where the quarterback would pass.

Pregnant pause.

"At?" said Scovil.

Kimball didn't speak.

"*At?*" Scovil persisted.

Kimball looked confused.

"*A-a-a-at?*" said Scovil.

Said Kimball: "Hell, I don't know. At BYU, I guess!"

* * * * *

Kimball was an unusual interview for any reporter. After transferring to Utah State, he declared that his goal was to win the national championship.

That was sort of unusual.

But there were other things. For instance, his "theme" days. When he was at BYU he would show up in full costume of someone famous, arriving for class dressed as Jim Morrison, the late, great lead singer of The Doors. He would have a guitar, sunglasses and a tie-dyed shirt. His most memorable impersonation was when he came dressed as Bjorn Borg, wearing tennis shorts, shirt, shoes and carrying a racquet. His hair was in a Borg-like terrycloth headband. He wore wristbands, tennis shoes—the whole routine.

Just to make it convincing, he spoke in a Swedish accent all day.

"He'd just keep this thing going all day or all week," said former teammate Blaine Fowler. "I'd be alone with him and I'd say, 'Come on, Gym, give it up.' He'd answer me in the accent. A true method actor."

"Beyond bizarre," is the way another former teammate put it. But always good for a laugh.

* * * * *

There is no way to talk about Kimball without mentioning the "blood letter."

After being at BYU a year, and seeing the long line of quarterbacks, Kimball decided it was time to move on. He wasn't listed number one or number two on the depth chart, so he transferred to USU.

But not before leaving his mark on BYU—in blood.

Stories have circulated for years about his "colorful" letters. Some say he wrote one after transferring to USU. He purportedly sent a 1983 missive, signed in his own blood, to Edwards, saying, "The day of vengeance has come." Kimball later said he doesn't recall sending any from Logan.

But he did remember sending one to Edwards when in high school.

Edwards remembered, too.

"He wrote me a letter in blood that said something about us being blood brothers for life. It had a skull and crossbones. It was all about him being excited to be at BYU and playing for us," said Edwards.

Said Kimball, "I remember hearing [assistant coach] Norm Chow seeing the letter and saying, 'What the hell is *this?*'"

* * * * *

For all the crazy antics McMahon performed, he didn't get fully warmed up until he went to the pros. Kimball, on the other hand, hit the ground running, the first time he set foot at BYU.

It seemed Kimball never ran out of gag material. Each day at a certain time, the campus chimes would play the national anthem, and students crossing the quad and other areas would stop and stand at attention. It was far from the football field, but close enough that the chimes could be heard in the distance.

One afternoon Kimball was hunched behind the center, awaiting a snap at practice, when the anthem sounded. Kimball, who was a scout-team quarterback, didn't miss a beat. He pulled back from the center, took off his helmet and stood at attention while the first-team defense fumed.

The coaches were calling at him to have the ball snapped, so practice could resume, but Kimball serenely remained until the last note had sounded.

It may have gone over well with the VFW, but not so with the coaches or defense.

\* \* \* \* \*

Drawing attention came naturally for Kimball. During one JV game, he and the rest of the Cougars were playing in a snowstorm. It was cold, wet, and fewer than a dozen fans were in the stands.

Late in the contest, with the outcome secured, Kimball stepped behind his center, then started clowning around. He looked left and right, then pulled back from the center. He cupped his hands around his ear-holes, pretending he couldn't hear due to the crowd noise. Then he signaled to an official that he couldn't hear. The official ordered Kimball to call for the snap.

Kimball complied, but not before he had done a fine imitation of a big-time quarterback in a big-time game.

All that was missing were the fans.

And the big-time game.

But the acting was superb.

\* \* \* \* \*

Teams aren't allowed by the NCAA to have full-blown practices during summers. But quarterbacks and receivers can get together on their own to practice their patterns and timing.

McMahon, Kimball, and receivers Plater and Jim Edwards had just finished a workout one summer day. Plater pulled off his sock and pointed to a gigantic blister on his foot.

Plater, who loved fooling around as much as Kimball, dared him to eat the blister.

Everyone laughed.

Then Plater said he'd pay Kimball $5 to eat it.

Much to the disgust of his teammates, he did.

Moral to the story: One man's blister is another man's lunch?

\* \* \* \* \*

Shawn Knight was a first-team All-Conference defensive tackle for the Cougars in 1983-86. He was also a player of enormous nervous energy—both on and off the field.

The Cougars had already wrapped up their conference championship early in 1985, but had one regular season game left: Hawaii. That meant the traditional flight to the Islands.

The drawback was the players rarely got a chance to enjoy beach life. Most of the time they were in their rooms studying or attending practice and film sessions—not a good formula for hyperactive types.

That year, Knight ended up on the balcony of one of the upper floors of the Princess Kaiulaini hotel on Waikiki Beach, confined to his room.

That's when Mike King, the team's business manager, started getting calls.

"It was the general manager of the hotel," recalled King. "He said they were getting complaints from tourists who said they were getting hit by water balloons."

Upon further investigation, he learned that Knight and another couple of players had rigged up a makeshift slingshot, comprised primarily of surgical tubing. They would rear back and launch the water balloons. Because of the strength of the players involved, "they were launching water balloons two or three blocks," said King.

When the balloons hit something, they didn't just bounce off.

King went up to Knight's room to talk to him. The evidence was clear. There in the room was a tangle of surgical tubing and the sliding door to the balcony was wide open. Not far away were several players, looking sheepish.

"We've been getting quite a few complaints about people getting hit with water balloons," began King.

Knight was mischievous, but not rebellious. He immediately shut down the artillery fire for the night.

\* \* \* \* \*

That wasn't Knight's first run-in with King and the authorities.

"He was just one of those energetic guys," said King.

A year earlier, there was another incident. Looking for something to pass the time while on the road, Knight decided to rent a moped to tour Oahu.

Fair enough, except for one thing: Somewhere during his tour, he decided to load another 300-pound player onto the same moped, giving an entirely new meaning to the term "stress management."

A few hours later King got a call from the rental agency. Knight had brought the moped back in time. But the motor was burned out.

"I told them at the agency that they saw Shawn and the other guy when they came in. They could see how big they were. I told them I didn't feel much responsibility…except to recommend they don't do that again," laughed King.

BYU ended up not being liable for the damage.

Meanwhile, Knight was admonished to never again try to test the laws of physics.

\* \* \* \* \*

Among the fine players and colorful characters in BYU history was linebacker Bob Davis, who played in the late 1980s.

Not only was he an outstanding player, but an outstanding quote. Writers inundated him on media days to see what he had to say. It was Davis who popularized the art of head-butting BYU teammates as a sign of approval.

Davis began experiencing shoulder problems one season. The training staff determined he had a joint that was arthritic from all his weight lifting. Often a cortisone shot would relieve the pain.

Davis was dispatched to the team doctor, who took the muscular player into his office. "Maybe this will help," said the doctor.

After administering the shot, the doctor said, "You don't look so well."

Davis was pale, but game. "I'm fine," he said.

He walked out of the office. Immediately the doctor and trainer heard a loud thud.

Davis had passed out and crashed into the wall.

Which proved an old theory of most sports medicine people. Break a finger, tear a ligament, sprain an ankle, no problem.

But show the kid a needle and he's a basket case.

\* \* \* \* \*

Another time the Cougars were in the locker room at half time, when some of the coaches heard screaming.

Not wailing. Not moaning.

Screaming.

"I hear that and I think someone's leg is being amputated," said one eyewitness who asked not to be identified.

As it turned out, the only thing happening was someone on the medical staff was administering a shot. Davis was receiving a painkiller after jamming a thumb. But it wasn't the injury that was making him scream. It was the shot.

Tough guys aren't always tough in all areas.

\* \* \* \* \*

John Hunter was imposing, just by his size. He also had a temper. It was a volatile combination.

That fact didn't escape the watchful eyes of Roger French, the Cougars' longtime offensive line coach.

French had a way of testing players. He would get to know them a little, ferret out the weakness in their approach to the game, and hammer away at that weakness until it became a strength.

It was a good philosophy—once everything had been worked out. Before that happened things could get complicated.

When Hunter arrived at BYU in the mid-1980s, it quickly become obvious he was intense. So French would needle him until he would snap. "I'm gonna kill him. I'll kill him!" Hunter would rage. French would reply, "I don't have time for you to kill me."

At one practice Hunter, an offensive tackle, became so frustrated he threw his helmet over a row of trees lining the field. It looked like he was launching a satellite.

Meanwhile, trainer George Curtis would act as a buffer, telling Hunter not to let the needling bother him. Gradually Hunter adapted.

During Hunter's senior season, the Cougars were playing at home. According to Curtis they had just scored, when Hunter— who had been learning to control his emotions for all four years at BYU—came charging to the sidelines where he met Curtis.

"George!" he said. "George, look at this!"

There was an enormous gob of expectorant—commonly known as a loogie—running down his face.

"I'll get a towel to wipe it off," said Curtis.

"No! No! Leave it!" Hunter shouted.

He ran down the sidelines until he found his nemesis, French. "Coach! Look!"

French looked to see the ghastly phlegm on his player's face.

Said Hunter, "Look! He [an opponent] did *this* and I didn't even slug him."

"That's really good," said French, shaking his head. "Now go clean it off."

Hunter had figured if he could allow an opponent to hock in his face and not lose his cool, he was in complete control.

And he was.

If you don't believe it, try it at home with your little brother.

\* \* \* \* \*

French was a bit of an amateur philosopher/motivator. Sometimes he seemed to want his sayings enshrined in history, like Knute Rockne or Vince Lombardi. Only too often it came out in some convoluted malapropism. For instance, he was known to say, "All right, guys, I want you to pair up in threes."

Players tell of French attempting to fire his team up before a game in the mid-1980s. He had gathered the group for a few words of advice, launching into a rather drawn-out story about harvesting potatoes. He told of machinery digging up the potatoes and dumping them into a truck. The truck then went to the processing plant. The processing plant was on a hill, and as the truck proceeded along the road, the potatoes shifted, with the larger ones rising to the top and the smaller ones falling to the bottom.

Just before sending the players out of the locker room, he shouted, "Go out there and be big potatoes!"

Most of the players took the field shaking their heads and thinking they could smell French fries.

For years afterward, the inside joke among players prior to games, and even in the huddle, was that they needed to be "big potatoes."

\* \* \* \* \*

French had other material besides potatoes.

He once told his unit before taking the field that it needed to "Get out there and tear them into little bits of rabbit!"

Again, it became a sort of sheepish rallying cry. Players would huddle on the field, call a play, and promise one another they would make rabbit pieces out of the opposition.

\* \* \* \* \*

Malapropisms, though, were French's (pardon the pun) bread and butter.

For instance, there was one game in Provo in the late '80s, when the team was struggling. French called the offensive line to the sidelines to explain it had lined up wrong.

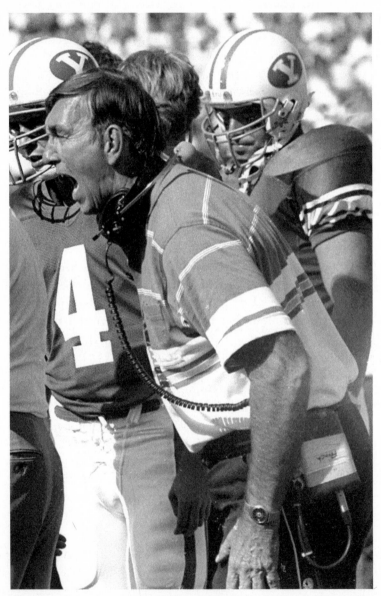

*Roger French admonished his players to be "big potatoes."*
*(Photo by Mark Philbrick, BYU Photo )*

"This is not rocket science," he said. "It's like a bank. You just have to have everything in the right place. You put the ones in with the ones, the tens in with the tens, the twenties in with the twenties and the forties in with the forties...it's real simple."

In honor of French, after a victory later that season, a lineman drew a picture of a $40 bill on the grease board in the locker room.

Across the bottom he wrote, "In French We Trust."

\* \* \* \* \*

French will forever be remembered at BYU for two things: his great technical skills as a coach, and as a quirky and unorthodox man.

They called him "The Creature."

French spent 21 years at BYU, yet rarely, if ever, established permanent residence. Most of the time his family remained at home in Minnesota; he would spend the school year in Provo.

The arrangement French had didn't always make for luxurious accommodations. Sometimes he slept in a motor home in Provo Canyon. Sometimes it was in a hotel. One year he stayed in a spare room at a nearby Lutheran church. But most of the time, players and coaches just assumed French slept in his coaching office.

How French got his nickname is unclear. The most commonly accepted explanation is that he would roll out of bed in his office for morning staff meetings, hair sticking up, face unshaven. He would walk to the water fountain, stick his comb down to get water on it, and comb back his hair.

When he first arose he looked like the creature from the Black Lagoon.

French wore his royal blue BYU polyester coaching pants and white belt in practice from the early 1980s, when they were in style, until he left BYU in 2001, when they looked like a wardrobe piece from *Saturday Night Fever.*

He was a wild man on the sidelines. He would play the profane but stirring speech from the movie *Patton* for his offensive linemen every year.

"You know what? I echo that man's sentiments," he would

say soberly.

The Creature was so superstitious that he would walk around the perimeter of the playing field for every game, hoping to find a lucky coin, then stick it in his socks (he also wore the same lucky socks for every game).

Fearful that French would be upset if he didn't find his coin, Chad Bunn, the former team video coordinator, and Duane Busby, the director of football operations, would get to the field before French left the locker room. They knew his pattern of walking around the perimeter of the grass or turf, just where it meets the grandstands. They would drop coins where they thought he would find them and then go sit in the stands to watch French come out of the locker room.

French would find his coin, and the game could go on.

\* \* \* \* \*

Speaking of superstitions, somewhere along the line—whether in college or the NFL, no one is exactly sure—Steve Young started collecting dirt.

His superstition was this: He would request dirt from the field on which he would be playing that day and have it brought to him in a paper cup. Then he would rub the dirt on his hands prior to the game. The idea was to get the feel of the place.

When the game was played on turf, Young had an alternate plan. He would dispatch a team manager to get dirt from one of the planters surrounding the stadium.

Did it work?

Just check the record.

\* \* \* \* \*

There are simple superstitions—like collecting dirt and coins—and then there are more taxing ones, like throwing up.

Todd Shell had that sort of superstition.

Shell was a ferocious linebacker for the Cougars in 1980-83. Early in his career he was young and nervous. He would get so worked up before games, he would ritually "hurl" in the locker room bathroom before taking the field.

By the time he was a senior, according to former teammate Tom Holmoe, Shell had accomplished so much that getting nervous enough to barf had become harder. But, as Holmoe puts it, "If he didn't throw up, he wasn't ready."

So he would try to work himself up to the point of nausea. He did so faithfully, every game.

Which makes a person wonder: Why didn't he pick an easier superstition like, say, rubbing a rabbit's foot?

\* \* \* \* \*

It's one thing to thrive in the face of adversity. It's admirable to take criticism and turn it into a positive.

But it's something else entirely to *ask* for it.

Bill Schoepflin was a cornerback for the famous 1980 team. He was a weight lifter in an era when not all cornerbacks wanted to lift weights.

One day he came to defensive backfield coach Dick Felt's office. Felt was talking with a booster when Schoepflin arrived. The booster offered to leave, but Schoepflin said it wasn't necessary.

"I just need to ask one question," he said.

And that was....

"You're not yelling at me."

"What?" said Felt.

"Am I doing something wrong? You're not getting after me."

"Bill," said Felt, "I don't need to yell at you."

Later Felt would say that was always Schoepflin's approach. He worked hard, expected to be pushed, and didn't like sliding by without someone challenging him.

Even if it meant asking for criticism.

\* \* \* \* \*

The Cougars embarked on a grueling non-conference schedule in 2000 that included games against Florida State, Virginia, Syracuse and Mississippi State.

But Coach Edwards wasn't against allowing his players to experience the areas in which they played. When they played at Virginia, he took the team to Monticello, home of Thomas Jefferson.

As they walked about the grounds, Margin Hooks, a receiver, was impressed. But not *that* impressed.

"Well, Margin, what do you think of Jefferson's place?" someone on the team said.

"Shoot," said Hooks. "I thought we were going to see George and Weezie's!"

\* \* \* \* \*

Coaches like French, Fred Whittingham and Tom Ramage were known tough guys.

But that doesn't mean they couldn't look silly on occasion.

Chad Bunn was a student manager with BYU in the mid-1980s, when the Cougars were at the Holiday Bowl. His job was to set up the projector so the players from the defensive unit could watch film.

One day they were having a film session, when the projector bulb went out. The bulbs on the old projectors would get white hot, and handlers needed to be careful to wait for them to cool before unscrewing them. Bunn went off to find a napkin or rag to undo the bulb. But Ramage couldn't wait. When Bunn got the top off the projector, Ramage reached in and tried to unscrew the hot bulb.

"Awwwwwwwww! "he howled in pain when his hand touched the bulb.

He quickly flipped the bulb away, as Bunn arrived and installed a new bulb.

"He's standing in front of the projector," said Bunn, "and Tom reaches back to see if the new bulb is in, looks down into the projector, turns the light on, and burns his eye—just—*toasts* his eye! There are tears pouring down his cheek and his burned hand is like a claw, his eye is all red. The players are all sitting there watching and trying not to laugh."

Even for tough guys, patience is a virtue.

\* \* \* \* \*

One more French connection. Or two.

The man was intense. "Pardon my French" wasn't just an expression.

He was animated and profane on the sidelines in his double-knit coaching pants, play sheet stuffed in front. On one occasion French was protesting to officials that BYU's kicker had been roughed. To demonstrate, he swung his leg up, imitating a kicker, and landed flat on his back.

It was an effective demonstration, right down to the part where he roughed himself up.

When Robbie Bosco and Blaine Fowler were freshman quarterbacks, they were standing on the sidelines, knowing they wouldn't get in the game. As usual, French was going crazy.

It was a key fourth-down play and the call was close. Fowler was walking down the sidelines when he stumbled over something.

"What was that?" he said to Bosco.

He looked down just in time to see French, prone on his stomach, his eye flush against the first-down marker, trying to line it up to see if the Cougars had made the first down.

On another occasion, French was watching a running play. As the Cougar back swept around the end and began charging up the sidelines, French began running alongside. In those days, the headsets were "hard wired" to a line. That didn't stop French. He charged downfield, trying to keep up with the Cougar running back so he could see the play unfold.

Suddenly, he reached the end of the line.

"It pulls him to a dead stop," recalls Fowler. As French walked back toward the team, players noticed French had blood on his mouth. The headset had raked across his face.

"Coach," said Bosco, "there's blood on your mouth."

"Oh yeah, well, when I yell really loud," retorted French, "my throat bleeds."

* * * * *

The Creature wasn't the only coach who could get worked up. Safeties coach Barry Lamb could get so agitated he was spitting blood, too.

It's just that in his case, it wasn't his own.

Hans Olsen, a former USU defensive lineman, recalled a day in practice when matters were becoming extremely intense. On one play, free safety Jason Walker got his fingers smashed between helmets and an enormous blood blister, half the size of a marble, appeared.

Walker went to Lamb and showed him the injury.

"Barry grabs Walker's finger," recalled Olsen, "and sticks it in his mouth. Then he *bites it*. It opens the blister and starts spurting on Barry's lips. He just spits it out and throws Walker's hand down and says, 'Get back in there!' "

* * * * *

Former NFL coach Mike Holmgren had a reputation as a tough guy, too. But that wasn't always the case. In fact, in the early years as an assistant at BYU, he was sort of a softie.

"He wasn't a tough guy, but he was trying to be a tough guy," said Fowler. "Back then it was like a big act. We'd push him to see how far we could push him."

Once after practice, Holmgren asked quarterback Robbie Bosco to stay late. As they stood on the northwest corner of the field, the rest of the team was leaving. Bosco remained behind. Holmgren began working on his tough guy routine.

"I'm going out the gate at the other end of the field and I can hear him screaming," said Fowler.

Next day, as Fowler arrived at the football office for a quarterbacks meeting, Holmgren called him over. "Blaine," he said. "I want to get your opinion. I didn't raise my voice the other day at Robbie, did I?"

*Is this a trick question?* Fowler thought.

"Yes," said Fowler.

"Aw, you are full of it," said Holmgren. "You are so full of it, I don't know why I even ask you. You guys are like joined at the hips. I don't know why I even asked you."

Fowler said Holmgren always had a soft heart. "He was too nice to be that way," he continued. "But he was working on being tough at BYU. He honed his craft there."

Sometimes tough guys just aren't born tough guys. They become that way.

* * * * *

Another of the true characters of BYU athletics was former football trainer Ollie Julkunen.

The longtime locker room fixture was known to be a master of the one-liner.

One year a BYU player got married in New Orleans in the off season. He sent wedding announcements to many of the football staff and players.

When Julkunen looked at the invitation, he noted something peculiar. Though the player was to be married in a Baptist church in Louisiana, the invitation had a picture of the Salt Lake LDS temple.

On a day when the player was on campus, Julkunen asked him where he got the picture for his wedding announcement.

"Oh, that's the church we're getting married in," he said.

When Julkunen told him that wasn't a New Orleans Baptist church, but an LDS temple, the player protested. "No. That's a church in New Orleans," he insisted.

Julkunen smiled and pointed to the statue of the Angel Moroni that adorns the top of many LDS temples.

"And I suppose," said Ollie, "that's Louie Armstrong."

On another occasion, Ollie and trainer George Curtis were walking behind business manager Mike King, who walked with a limp, due to a childhood bout with polio.

Julkunen said to Curtis, "George, how tall do you think Mike King is?"

"Oh, I don't know," said Curtis. "Maybe five-eight."

Julkunen was silent for a moment as they walked behind King, who was listening with a smile as he walked ahead.

Said Ollie: "Five-six. Five-eight. Five-six. Five-eight."

\* \* \* \* \*

John Neal was an all-conference safety at BYU in 1977 and 1979. He was tough. He was mean.

And he was not the least bit interested in taking it easy on an entertainer who happened to want to do a *Paper Lion* scene.

It was 1977, and Donny and Marie fever was still in force. The Osmonds had a television variety show going strong. One of the plans was for Donny to film a segment for the show, in which he would play wide receiver and race downfield through the defense.

BYU's defensive players got good news and bad news. The good news was they would be on national television. The bad news: They would be missing tackles all over the field. They had been instructed to miss Osmond on purpose, allowing him to score a long touchdown.

The TV crew arrived for the filming, and Edwards told his players what they were to do. "Nobody tackle him," said Edwards.

Neal wasn't listening.

He heard, but he wasn't listening.

The play was called, the cameras rolled, and Osmond came over the middle, catching the pass on the run. But just as he caught the ball, Neal nailed him with a chest-high tackle, separating the singer from the football in short order. Osmond was knocked flat. Some thought he was knocked out. One thing is certain: When he got up, he did so slowly.

You might say he had an amazing Technicolor dream.

In one of the few incidents when Edwards was honestly upset, he called out, "I told you not to touch that guy!"

Neal tried to look contrite but didn't quite get it done. Because nobody came across the middle on Neal unchallenged.

Even if he did have his own TV show.

\* \* \* \* \*

Chris Hoke was a typically big defensive lineman.

But so big that it embarrassed him?

The Cougars traveled to Fresno to play the Bulldogs in 1998. For several days the Cougars had been discussing what a loud-mouthed crowd attended Fresno State games.

"Everyone kept warning us they were probably the worst fans we would ever face," said Hans Olsen, who played on that BYU team. "They would really get drunk and they were horrible."

As kickoff time neared, Hoke and Olsen, a pair of defensive linemates, were standing on the sidelines getting ready to go in, when the fans began to chant. At first the players weren't sure what was being said. Hoke, who wore No. 58, said to Olsen, "Hans, what are they saying?"

"Um, I think they're saying, 'Fifty-eight, lose some weight!'" said Olsen.

Hoke looked crestfallen.

"Pretty soon, he starts getting emotional," recalled Olsen.

When they got on the field and huddled, Hoke brought up the chant again.

"Hoke is looking at me in the huddle," said Olsen, "and he says, 'Do you think it's the jersey that makes me look fat?' I said, 'Don't listen to them.' He said, 'Well, they wouldn't say it if they didn't think it.'

"We got through the series and end up back on the sidelines. Hoke is still getting emotional. He's trying to suck in his gut. I'm like, 'Hoke, that's not going to help.' He's saying, 'I'm not going back on the sidelines.'"

According to Olsen, for the next two weeks back in Provo, Hoke continued to be upset about the insensitive taunts.

"He was really upset, watching what he was eating," said Olsen.

History in the making: A defensive lineman on a diet.

\* \* \* \* \*

Ever dream you went to school without your clothes? There are worse dreams than that.

For instance, going to a football game without your helmet.

The 2000 Cougars traveled to Jacksonville, where they played a game against Florida State. In the two weeks leading up to the game, Olsen was repeatedly bothered by a dream in which he was on the field, sans helmet and cleats. The dream occurred three or four times.

Olsen didn't mention it to anyone until a few days before kickoff. He told Hoke, "Chris, I keep having this weird dream. I keep dreaming I left my helmet and cleats home for the game."

"Me too," said Hoke.

They were creeped out to find they had both been having the same dream.

The players decided they couldn't let their dreams affect their game, so they went to Edwards to explain the situation.

They made an appointment to meet with him the next day. When they walked into his office, they spotted his well-used brown leather couch. Hoke laid down on the couch, like a patient in a psychiatrist's office.

"Coach," said Hoke, "I've been having some dreams and need some help. I keep dreaming we've left our helmets and cleats back home."

Olsen said he was having the same problem.

Recalled Olsen, "Coach told us, 'I'm not a psychiatrist. Maybe you should talk to [associate A D] Pete Witbeck.'" (Not surprisingly, neither was Witbeck.)

Then the longtime coach assured them he would assign some equipment people to be sure the two defensive tackles got their equipment on the plane to Florida.

They never did go to see Witbeck.

But they never lost track of their equipment, either.

\* \* \* \* \*

When Olsen was a sophomore, he wanted to play. Bad. And he didn't want to wait.

Olsen was a backup that year, along with teammates Hoke, Setema Gali and Ifo Pili. It wasn't as though they never played. In fact, it might have been that they played too much. That just made them want more field time.

In the San Diego State game, the foursome hadn't been rotated into the lineup, which didn't sit well with them. They felt they had played well in the previous eight games. Why sit now?

"We felt we had done well to that point, maybe even better than the starters, so when we didn't get in, we started getting obnoxious, complaining to each other, hoping [defensive line coach] Tom Ramage would hear. But we go out in the second half, and we still don't get in the game," said Olsen.

The next week, Olsen—still miffed about not playing—hatched a plan. "I said to the other guys, 'If I'm not going to play in the games, I'm not sitting through film. Let's get ourselves kicked out of the film session.'"

It was a good plan—become disruptive enough to get tossed. They all agreed.

On Monday the film period began, and the defensive players were all sitting in the room, while Ramage turned on the videotape replay. One play came on, involving starter Issiah Magalei, so Olsen made a wise comment. "Great tackle, Issiah," he said.

He looked around for support from the other players.

Nothing.

Another play came up involving starter Daren Yancey.

"Boy, Daren, you looked tired. Looks like you needed some help out there," Olsen said.

This continued for several minutes. Still nothing from Olsen's cohorts.

Finally, Ramage stood and said, "That's it. I'm sick of this, I'm sick of your talk. Get out of here!" he said to Olsen.

As he walked out the door, Olsen whispered to his partners in crime. "Where were you guys? Come on!" But nobody spoke.

Olsen ended up the only one missing the film session.

"They left me twisting in the wind," recalled Olsen. "I thought we were all in it together. I ended up being the only one in trouble."

A week or so later, Olsen told Ramage about the pact to get kicked out of the film session.

The power of one.

In this case, only one.

\* \* \* \* \*

Anyone who grew up in snow country remembers the peculiar joy of having a "snow day" in which school gets unexpectedly canceled.

For everyone else, there was Carlos Nuno.

From 1997-99, the Cougar tight end had a routine at practice that he never quite gave up. As players were dressing during two-a-days, Nuno would burst through the locker room door and call out, "Practice is canceled! Let's all go home!" The first few times he did it, he was met with excited looks—not unlike kids getting out of school in winter. But after a few tries, nobody paid attention.

That didn't discourage him.

"The first two weeks of the season, guys would start taking their shoes off when he'd do that," recalled Olsen. "But he continued that through the entire season.."

\* \* \* \* \*

The 1998 Cougars were playing at Washington in a big game. Playing Washington was always a big game.

The contest was close. On a third-and-eight situation, Nuno got the call. He raced downfield and quarterback Kevin Feterik zoomed a perfect pass. But Nuno inexplicably dropped it.

When he came to the sidelines, his friend Olsen said, "Dang, Carlos, when we were eating breakfast I thought you were buttering toast, not your fingers."

\* \* \* \* \*

Freshmen. Gotta love 'em. Especially if you like practical jokes.

Chuck Cutler was a Cougar wide receiver in 1986-88. After he had been with the Cougars two or thee years, he devised a gimmick to entertain himself, at the expense of the freshmen.

Thursdays were days when the Cougars would practice in half-pads, meaning shorts, combined with shoulder pads and jersey. Cutler, though, would storm into the training room complaining about the coaches. "Doggone those coaches!" he would rant. "They're making us wear full pads today!"

Then he would storm out.

Upon hearing Cutler's complaining, the freshmen would all put on their full pads and lumber out to the practice field. Cutler would be out waiting for them in shorts, laughing at his private practical joke.

# Chapter 7

## *The Utah Game*

For sheer animosity, no game is more important each year than the one against Utah.

The rivalry has often gone beyond football and become personal. Though players on the teams are often friends—having competed in high school and attended camps together—the fans have always had a knack for taking it to the extreme.

Coaches and players recalled being on the team bus in the late 1970s at Utah, parked on the east side of the stadium, where students would congregate on game days. Several times one day the students began rocking the bus, threatening to overturn it.

Interestingly, that sort of behavior didn't intimidate the Cougars, it motivated them. LaVell Edwards often said he never had to do anything to get his team ready for the Utes—their fans would do it for him.

Ann Cannon, Edwards's daughter, recalled sitting in the stands, where Ute fans would quickly discover the coach's wife, Patti. Soon there were derogatory remarks made and things thrown at her.

One year she had taken so much abuse, she smacked a fan in the nose with her handbag, giving him a nosebleed. As Patti and her family left the area, the man, who was more than a little drunk, kept saying, "Coach Edwards' wife hit me. She hit me in the nose."

Right.

And consider yourself lucky, pal.

Hell hath no fury like a coach's wife after a personal remark.

\* \* \* \* \*

For more than 20 years BYU dominated the series with Utah.

But that didn't keep Ute fans from planning for the annual game.

The year 1980 was no exception. BYU came into the game needing a win to claim the WAC championship outright. Utah came in with the plan it usually had—to upset its biggest rival.

That year went the way a lot of them did in the '70s and '80s, with BYU 56-6.

Through the entire game, a contingent of fans near the Cougar bench was screaming obscenities. Jim McMahon, never intimidated by obscenities, seemed to thrive on it. After he threw for one touchdown, he looked squarely at the hecklers in the stands at Rice (now Rice-Eccles) Stadium, then pointed up at the scoreboard.

Enough said.

Some believe that was the first time anyone had used that particular type of in-your-face gesture at a college game. This much is certain: It became very popular in the years since.

Trash talkers everywhere can thank a group of Ute fans for making it possible.

\* \* \* \* \*

One of the big motivational tools the Cougars used over the years was the one supplied by team manager Mel Farr.

The five-feet-two Farr was small but strong. Before the biggest games of the season, he would do something the players loved: tear a city phone book in half. It was part wrist strength, part a technique of manipulating the pages so they could be torn in small bits at a time. But the technique never failed to inspire. He fired up the team in 1980 at the Holiday Bowl, just before the Cougars won their first ever bowl game. In fact, he did it before several bowl games.

And he always did it before the traditional rivalry game with Utah.

The year 1988 was no exception. The Cougars had struggled that year, and finished the season tied for third. Going into the Utah game they had lost an important contest at San Diego State. Earlier in the season they had lost at Wyoming.

*Jim McMahon may have started the trend of
pointing to the scoreboard to quiet hostile crowds.
(Photo by Mark Philbrick, BYU Photo)*

But with a bowl game still possible, and the contest with the Utes ahead, it seemed a good time to recruit Farr's particular talent.

The team had gathered the night before the game for its traditional cheeseburger dinner, and the coaching staff called on Farr. He seemed confident enough. But on that night, something wasn't right. He twisted. He pulled. He grunted.

Players chanted, "Mel! Mel! Mel!" as usual.

His face reddened. His veins bulged. Sweat beaded his forehead.

Still he couldn't work his way through the book.

Seconds turned to minutes. After more than half an hour, the players were still watching. Eventually, they started to get uncomfortable.

Mel worked on.

Finally, in a rare admission, Farr confessed—his fingers could no longer do the walking.

The next day, the Cougars went to Rice Stadium and got waxed 57-28 by the Utes—their first win over BYU in 10 years.

"That was the last time we ever had someone tear a phone book," said Mike King, BYU's associate athletics director/finance.

Even the best of charms eventually lose their magic.

\* \* \* \* \*

This has nothing to do with the Utah game, except to explain how Mel Farr and phone books became a tradition.

He began tearing books upon request at the 1980 Holiday Bowl. That year, the team held a meeting the night before the game. McMahon was in front of the group, conducting the proceedings. Someone mentioned he had heard Mel the manager could tear a San Diego phone book in half. Before long, the players were chanting, "We want Mel!"

After a bit of coaxing, Mel obliged.

As he got up on the stand at the hotel meeting room, he began working on the phone book, tugging, pulling, twisting and soon enough, sweating. The players watched at rapt attention, but as the time wore on...15 minutes...20 minutes...25 minutes. He

*Mel Farr (bottom center) was among the first to congratulate
LaVell Edwards after the 1980 Holiday Bowl.
(Photo by Mark Philbrick, BYU Photo)*

struggled to finish.

Feeling sympathetic toward him, McMahon came up to the diminutive Farr and said, "Here, Mel, let me help you."

Bad decision.

Mel swung his arm up, catching McMahon across the chest and knocking him back off the stand. The players howled. Mel perspired.

After over half an hour, he finally finished working his way through the book. He threw it in the air, pages fluttering to the floor. The players went nuts, cheering and pounding him on the back.

A tradition was born that wouldn't end until that day in 1988 when he couldn't get through the phone book, and Utah got a win.

\* \* \* \* \*

On the field—and even above it—the best-laid plans sometimes didn't work when it came to the big game.

For instance, in the early 1970s the game against Utah wasn't decided until the late minutes. A hot air balloon had been docked in the south end of Cougar Stadium, which had no bleachers in that era. A sudden gust of wind rose and dislodged the balloon. It wafted into the stadium.

The balloon continued over the marching band, which was in the end zone, gathering as the end of the game neared. The gondola whacked band members in the head and arms, then got snagged on the goal post.

"The Utah trainer was out there on the field with scissors, trying to cut it free," recalled Tom Ramage, a longtime BYU assistant coach.

Eventually the balloon was deflated. The grounds crew wadded it up and hauled it off.

"I kind of had to ask the question if someone had scored, would they have had to go to the other end for the extra-point kick?" said Ramage.

* * * * *

Nobody seems to remember the player or the year, just the quote.

After a loss to Utah in Provo, a BYU defensive player was near the goal post, trying keep it from being torn down by jubilant Ute fans.

One of the coaches said, "If he had protected the goal line during the game, he wouldn't have had to do it afterward!"

* * * * *

This isn't indicative of all recruiting wars. But it is indicative of LaVell Edwards.

In the early 1970s, Edwards was a little-known assistant coach at BYU. One of his responsibilities that year was to recruit a defensive lineman from Salt Lake City named Paul Linford.

As it neared time to commit to a school, Linford wavered between Utah and BYU. Eventually he devised a way to test the situation. He would call each school and say he wasn't going there. Then he would await the reaction.

On the day he made the calls, he first reached Edwards on the phone. He said he appreciated the effort, but he was going to attend Utah. Edwards responded that he hated to hear the news, but Linford was "a wonderful young man" and a "classy guy." Edwards then told him, "if you ever need anything, be sure and call me, you're such a fine young man," and wished him luck in his career at Utah.

Linford then called a Utah assistant coach who had recruited him, to say he was going to BYU. The Utah coach swore at him, calling him "an idiot" and said, "You'll be playing for a losing program. I can't believe they even like you."

Linford hung up the phone and called BYU again. This time he had a different answer. He told Edwards he had changed his mind.

All it took was a little unfriendly persuasion.

\* \* \* \* \*

Tom Holmoe, BYU's athletics director, was a legendary defensive back for the Cougars. He went on to a successful career in the NFL, both as a player and an assistant coach. Later he became head football coach at Cal-Berkeley, before returning to BYU to work in the athletic department.

Holmoe said even though a player moves on to other things, he never forgets his old college rivalries. In his case, that included the one with Utah.

In early and mid-1990s, Utah was finally starting to make the rivalry a close one. The Utes won three straight, four of five and five of seven games between the schools.

This only served to make the wagering more interesting.

Holmoe was an assistant coach for the San Francisco 49ers, when one year he began teasing with quarterback Steve Young, and Niners coach George Seifert—a former Utah player—as to who would win the upcoming rivalry game. One thing led to another until Seifert proposed a bet: If Utah won the annual game, Young and Holmoe would join the University of Utah's Crimson Club for a year. If BYU won, Seifert would join the Cougar Club.

Utah won that year.

"I don't know about Steve," said Holmoe, "but I joined the Crimson Club for a year. I was a card-carrying Cougar Club and Crimson Club member for one year."

For several years after, Holmoe would tease Seifert about the persistence of the Crimson Club, which continued to contact him, asking him to re-register as a member.

"I kept telling George, 'Your people just will not let me go!'" said Holmoe.

Once a Ute, always a Ute.

Whether you want to be or not.

\* \* \* \* \*

Thing about the Utah game was that you didn't ever want to get into a dispute with the fans. It wasn't worth the aggravation.

*LaVell Edwards and Utah coach Ron McBride were
the coaches when the rivalry finally became even.
(Photo by Mark Philbrick, BYU Photo)*

Former trainer Marv Roberson learned that the hard way.

In the 1970s, the Cougars were playing at what is now Rice-Eccles Stadium. A large, hostile crowd had gathered to watch the Utes lose one of many games in that era to the Cougars.

Pete Witbeck, then a Cougar assistant athletic director, had often told the players not to exchange snipes with the fans. "I would always tell them, 'Don't look at the fans. Don't give them that option, because you can't win!'" recalled Witbeck, who died in 2010.

But that year, Roberson couldn't help himself. A group of fans began taunting the Cougars, and Roberson responded by exchanging insults. Before long, the expected happened: Someone threw a whiskey bottle, catching Roberson in the head.

He was helped into the locker room to have his head stitched up.

It was one of the more unlikely scenes in college football—the trainer getting stitches while the players looked on.

\* \* \* \* \*

Despite the intensity, the Utah-BYU rivalry didn't really get close until the 1990s.

For the first 50 or so years, the rivalry was all in Utah's favor. The next 25 years or so went to BYU. But finally, the outcome started to be in doubt in the '90s.

Through the 1970s and '80s, BYU players often said playing Utah was "just another game on the schedule." By the 1990s it had suddenly become the biggest game of the season.

"I just know," said former Cougar Hans Olsen, "that everyone felt if we didn't win a single game the whole season, and we beat Utah, it was a successful season. We would go into the game feeling like that, too. It was always an amazing game."

Olsen was on the defensive line in 1998 when Ute kicker Ryan Kaneshiro missed a last-minute chip-shot field goal to allow BYU the victory. As he lined up, Olsen was screaming, "You're gonna miss this one! You're gonna miss!"

"I could see him sweating," recalled Olsen. "He wasn't a very cool, calm guy. The more you see a guy sweat, the louder you get with him, so we turned it up. I don't know how much that had to do with him missing, but we turned it up."

\* \* \* \* \*

OK, so love does conquer all.

Even football.

A case in point was that of Brandon Doman, BYU's starting quarterback in 2000, the year the Cougars won their first 12 games.

Doman began dating Alisha Barker when he was a student at Skyline High in Salt Lake City. Big problem. She was a dyed-in-the-wool Ute.

After serving an LDS mission, Doman returned to play at BYU and resumed dating her. They became engaged. Problem number one: She wanted to have their wedding reception in the press box area at the University of Utah's Rice-Eccles Stadium.

Great view, but for a BYU quarterback, there sure was a lot of red in the house.

Eventually she convinced him to have the event in the home of the Utes. "It was just strange seeing the pictures of the Utah football players on the wall," Doman told the *Deseret News*. "It was fun."

The BYU coaches came to the reception dressed in blue, just to make a point.

As a sort of peace offering, the reception included an ice sculpture with an interlocking U and Y.

# Chapter 8

## *A Championship Season*

Sometimes good breaks just happen. Other times, teams don't wait for chance.

The 1984 BYU Cougars didn't wait.

It was an odd thing, in a way. The Cougars were picked to win the WAC that year, as usual, but nobody expected them to be phenomenal. They had gone 11-1 the previous year, but they had a new starting quarterback in Robbie Bosco, who had the unenviable job of trying to make people forget Steve Young.

It didn't appear they were headed for an unforgettable year. They opened at Pittsburgh, which was ranked No. 3 in the nation. They had what was expected to be a tough game against Baylor. Their annual grudge matches with Hawaii and Utah were on the road.

Winning the conference championship? Even with a new quarterback, they felt that was a good possibility. But a national championship? Please. Only one person had that in mind.

Offensive lineman Craig Garrick, a team captain, intended from the start to capitalize on BYU's Top 10 ranking the previous year. While most experts believed the Cougars would be merely a big fish in a mid-major pond, the emotional Garrick had other ideas. During the summer of 1984 he mailed out a letter to teammates, urging them to go undefeated. It was his way of getting an early start.

The play that determined the season, as much as any other, was Kyle Morrell's goal-line tackle in Hawaii, in which he vaulted over the offensive line and tackled Warrior quarterback Raphel Cherry from behind, dragging him down on the spot. It was a

*The 1984 Cougars collected many memories on
their way to a national championship.
(Photo by Mark Philbrick, BYU Photo)*

phenomenal play, bordering on unbelievable.

Interestingly, Morrell and teammates seemed to be certain a play like that would happen.

"We just totally expected something was going to happen," said Jim Edwards, a member of that team and son of the coach. "It was our destiny, we felt, to go undefeated. So when Kyle made that play, everybody knew that was one of the greatest defensive plays in the history of BYU, but everybody just expected someone to step up. It's like we kind of didn't realize how great it was until the game was over. When we saw the film, and realized how close that game was...

"From then on," continued the younger Edwards, "we just lined up on plays and waited to see what happened."

When you have destiny on your shoulder, usually what happens is good.

\* \* \* \* \*

As shocking as it was that BYU could actually win a national championship, the realization began to settle in, slowly but surely as the season progressed. With each passing win, hopes rose.

The Cougars had moved to the No. 3 spot nationally late in the year. But they knew Nebraska had to lose to Oklahoma and South Carolina would have to lose to 3-5-1 Navy to pave the way for them to move into the top position.

On Nov. 24, BYU traveled to Salt Lake to defeat a determined Utah, 24-14. Utah State was the last opponent left on the schedule. As the team bus drove south out of Salt Lake County and passed Point of the Mountain, the team was listening to the Oklahoma-Nebraska game on the radio.

Just then, the bus passed a business beside the freeway with a banner that said, "BYU, National Champions!" At the same moment, the results of the Oklahoma game came in—Oklahoma had won.

The players burst into cheers.

"From then on, we were thinking we could do it," said former associate athletics director/finance Mike King. "We went into the

Michigan [Holiday Bowl] game pretty confident that we could win the championship. And we did."

*  *  *  *  *

Actually, it was Garrick who first raised the specter of a national title.

"I remember it vividly," said former return star Vai Sikahema. "It was the first time anyone ever uttered the words 'national championship' on our team."

It was the night before the game against Pittsburgh. Nobody, to that point, had even thought of a championship—nobody except Garrick.

At the team meeting, Garrick stood and said, in effect, "Men, if we win tomorrow, we will run the table and play for the national championship in December."

Talk is cheap. Is there a team captain in the country who doesn't give some sort of speech on the eve of the first game? Most of the players didn't take the challenge seriously. Some may have just chalked it up to bravado or "captain talk." Some don't remember.

But Sikahema went home and wrote it in his journal.

"From then on, it was a steady climb," recalled Sikahema.

A climb to a place no other BYU team had been before or since.

*  *  *  *  *

The national championship was on the line during the 1984 Holiday Bowl. Bosco got hurt in the first quarter when a Michigan player rolled on his ankle. Bosco's cleat had been caught in the turf on the play and he ended up with a sprained ankle and twisted knee.

Doctors took him to the locker room for an exam.

"One question," said Bosco. "If I get hit again, will it do more serious damage to the leg?"

The answer he was waiting for arrived: no.

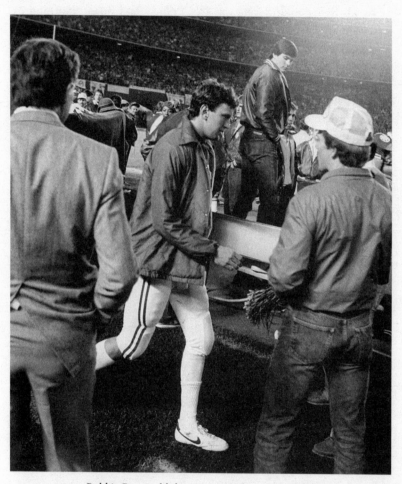

*Robbie Bosco told doctors to tape him up and send
him back in during the 1984 Holiday Bowl.
(Photo by Mark Philbrick, BYU Photo)*

"Tape me up," he said.

Doctors taped Bosco from mid-thigh to ankle. As he came through the tunnel at Jack Murphy Stadium, he was met halfway by his father, asking if he was OK. "Fine," said Bosco. Nothing a little tape couldn't fix.

When he walked onto the field, the crowd roared. Even as he warmed up, he wasn't sure he could go. But the adrenaline rush provided by the crowd overcame the worries.

On his first play back, a Michigan lineman caught him in the knee again. When the Cougar offensive linemen saw what happened, they told Bosco in the huddle, "That won't happen again."

"Rest of the game, almost three quarters, I was in the pocket and nobody touched me," said Bosco. "Our line took great pride in protecting the quarterback."

\* \* \* \* \*

The big debate that year in the media was whether the Cougars—who played in the lightly regarded Western Athletic Conference—deserved to be considered the No. 1 team. It was a subject of discussion for several weeks.

Another item of discussion was the difference between coaches. At the time, the BYU football coach was LaVell Edwards and the basketball coach was Ladell Andersen.

Val Hale, BYU's athletic director from 1999-2004, remembered listening to a national radio show, driving home one night. The broadcasters were discussing the matter of a national championship when one of the announcers said, "You know, I don't think Ladell Edwards gets the credit he deserves!"

*The final score told it all in the 1984 Holiday Bowl—*
*BYU was national champion.*
*(Photo by Mark Philbrick, BYU Photo)*

# Chapter 9

## *Odds and Ends*

It gets cold on the high plains of Laramie, Wyoming during football season, even in the early fall. Sometimes it can get downright scary.

And always it's hostile.

Jeff Blanc was a Cougar running back in the mid-1970s, a colorful, emotional player who led the Cougars in rushing three straight seasons. BYU was playing at Wyoming during his junior season and, naturally, there was snow on the ground when the team arrived at the stadium. As BYU moved onto the field for pregame warm-ups, Wyoming fans were carrying placards, taunting the Cougars. Quickly, it progressed to snowball tossing.

Eventually, one of the snowballs hit Blanc in the ear-hole of his helmet. Though he showed no strong emotion to the crowd, when assistant coach Garth Hall looked over, he could see Blanc was heading toward the stands—and the person who threw the iceball.

"At that moment," recalled Hall, "he was ready to kill someone."

Hall walked over to the star running back, only to discover "he's got that far-away look in his eyes, so I spend 10 minutes calming him down."

Eventually Hall talked Blanc out of going into the stands and reminded him to focus on the game—which he did spectacularly. Blanc ran for 215 yards, which was, at the time, the third-best rushing day in BYU history. The Cougars won 33-20.

"It all started with a snowball," said Hall.

Meanwhile, it served as a lesson: Don't throw snowballs, you

*Jeff Blanc had a career day after getting hit in the ear by a snowball.*
*(Photo by Mark Philbrick, BYU Photo)*

could put out someone's eye. Or you just might motivate him to run over your team all afternoon.

\* \* \* \* \*

"Dress for the weather," your mother used to say. That's sometimes harder than it sounds.

Ted Tollner was a BYU assistant coach in 1981. The previous year he had coached at San Diego State. When the Aztecs went to Laramie to play, they had arrived with sweatshirts and sweatpants under their uniforms. The guys from the beach were preoccupied with staying warm.

As it turned out, they got wiped out anyway. They had spent more time worrying about the cold than about the Cowboys.

The next year Tollner told that story to the Cougars, saying his San Diego State team had gone to Laramie "looking like a bunch of snow bunnies." He vowed not to overreact this time.

"We're going up there with our usual jerseys and we're not going to worry about the cold, and we're going to kick their butts," said Tollner.

When the game began, it was crisp and cold, but no snow. Soon it became overcast. As the second quarter arrived, so did the snow. In a five-minute period, the field was covered. The grounds crew began shoveling to clear the yard stripes.

Meanwhile, the Cougars were on the field with no extra warmth. They were wearing just their normal uniforms.

True to Tollner's vow, they didn't overreact. They faithfully avoided looking like "snow bunnies." But they did freeze. They had no sideline jackets, warmer jerseys or hand warmers. Once their sweat cooled, it turned icy and they began to feel and look a bit like frozen yogurt.

"I've never been so cold in my life," said Hall.

Final score: Wyoming 33, Non-Snow Bunnies 20.

\* \* \* \* \*

It's a good thing to avoid trouble.

But occasionally, it's nice to just plow over it.

*In Laramie, Wyoming, the snow could be a
problem at almost any time of the season.
(Photo by Mark Philbrick, BYU Photo)*

When Chuck Cutler was playing for the Cougars in the late 1980s, the team was required to walk through a stadium concourse at Wyoming to get to the locker room. That year, the Cougars filed through the tunnel to a chorus of boos from fans, then into the concourse. An obviously drunken fan approached Cutler, stuck his face up, and proceeded to yell obscenities.

Cutler made a move to the left, but the fan stepped over and continued swearing. Cutler moved to the right. Same results.

He made a last attempt at getting around the obnoxious fan. No deal.

So he made one more move, head-butting the guy.

That might not have done much damage, except Cutler was wearing his helmet. His facemask caught the fan on the bridge of his nose, splitting it wide open.

That time he let Cutler pass.

"I don't know if he even knew what happened," said Cutler. "But I'll bet the next morning he was wondering."

\* \* \* \* \*

Cutler didn't believe in talking about his accomplishments, even though he had a record-setting career. He was modest to a fault.

One of the records he set was for consecutive games with at least one touchdown reception. That year, he was set to break the record in a game against New Mexico. Paul James, the longtime BYU announcer, came down on the field before kickoff and said, "How does it feel, about to tie the record today?" said James.

"What record?" said Cutler.

"Don't you know?" James said.

"No."

"The record for consecutive games with at least one touchdown pass."

Though Cutler did tie the record, the following game he failed to score.

After his playing career, Cutler worked briefly as a color

commentator with James. One afternoon James asked a trivia question on the air: "Who caught the first pass from Ty Detmer?"

"Who do you think it was, Chuck?" James said after several wrong guesses had been phoned in.

Cutler only shook his head.

"Come on, Chuck," said James. "Who caught his first pass?"

"Uh. Matt Bellini?" said Cutler.

By then, James was becoming annoyed.

"Let's pause now for a commercial break," said James.

During the break James said, "C'mon, Chuck! Just tell 'em it's you."

Cutler was dumbfounded. "Paul, I didn't know it was me."

Records might be made to be broken, but in some cases, they're made to be forgotten.

* * * * *

He never did like that radio show.

Cutler continued his assignment, filling in for regular Marc Lyons, who was coaching high school at the time and couldn't be at all the games. He especially didn't like the postgame call-in show.

One Saturday he was tired after the game, and asked James if he could go home early. He had already done several games that year and noticed a trend. None of the questions were directed to him. LaVell Edwards would join them, and all the queries would go to the head coach.

James told Cutler to go ahead and leave. What could it hurt?

Cutler took the elevator to ground level, found his car, and began driving home.

First caller: "This question is for Chuck."

Said Cutler, "I had probably done six games and not a single question was for me. Then the one time I leave early, the moment I get in the car, the first question is for me."

In matters of national security and radio broadcasting, never leave your post.

\* \* \* \* \*

It's a temptation to assume it was all football, all the time in the LaVell Edwards household. Not so. For the most part, Edwards didn't talk shop at home.

That doesn't mean his wife, Patti, had to refrain. In fact, she was more inclined to talk football around the dinner table.

Patti's involvement in her husband's career could sometimes cause angst. For instance, in the early 1970s, the Cougars were in Logan. It was a hotly contested game that ended up with Utah State winning. Edwards handled the loss OK. Patti didn't.

"She really came uncorked," recalled her daughter, Ann.

At the time, Ann was a senior in high school—an age when seeing your mother lose her cool is, like, *sooooo* uncool.

"I said, 'You better rein it in or you're going to embarrass us,'" said Ann. "She said, 'You little brat! You better find your own way down the canyon!' and stomped off."

Ann wandered around the field for a while, wondering how to get home. She found the coach and asked if she could ride the team bus back to Provo. Patti was still mad.

LaVell decided he should drive the family car home.

"She was chewing him out for being stupid, and she was still mad at me," recalled Ann. "So that night in my journal I wrote how embarrassing it all was, why does she have to do that in public, etc. Now as a parent, I understand. But Dad came in my room the next day and said he thought he better have a look at what I wrote in the journal about my mother. Then he told me I probably should consider ripping the pages out.

"That was very much my dad. He was always very calm."

Her mom?

Calm, as well.

As long as she thought the officiating was fair.

\* \* \* \* \*

Sometimes, if you were an Edwards, being the center of attention went with the territory. For instance, the day in 1980 that Ann gave birth to a daughter was also the day the Cougars drubbed UTEP 83-7.

Ann was at a Salt Lake hospital, in the delivery room, in full labor. To her dismay, the Cougar game was on television in the same room.

At halftime her brother, mother and father all called to check on her to see how the delivery was going. Someone taking the calls at the nursing station asked, "Who is this Ann person? Every time someone calls, it sounds like there is a football game going on in the background?"

Which, of course, there was.

The moment word got out the coach's daughter was in the delivery room, it quickly filled with doctors, interns, nurses and medical students of all types.

And maybe a couple of pink ladies and a candy striper, for all she knew.

"Suddenly," she said, "I'm the number one spectator sport. They should have sold tickets."

The worst part, she added, is that "I wasn't at my best angle."

As it turned out, both she and the Cougars delivered spectacularly.

* * * * *

In all the years of football, the Edwards family rarely, if ever, missed one particular tradition: Patti's game-day stew.

Whenever the Cougars played at home she would make the stew for the family, no matter what time the kickoff. She was superstitious in that sort of way. She would change the sheets on certain days, organize things, etc.

So naturally the stew just had to happen.

Sometimes, if it was a late game, they would eat beforehand. Other times they would eat afterward. The philosophy went something like this: If Patti's stew was cooking, so were the Cougars.

*Patti was always behind LaVell, and often took defeats harder than he did.
(Photo by Mark Philbrick, BYU Photo)*

"We'd sit around the kitchen and talk about the game," said Ann. "Occasionally we'd turn on the call-in show to listen to my dad, but then somebody (usually my brother or I) would get so frustrated by the level of caller idiocy that we'd stomp over to the radio and rip off the knob."

So for those who love stew—or simply love BYU football—here's the highly successful game-day stew recipe:

### Patti's Game Day Stew

Serves 6-8
1 pound stew meat
4-6 carrots, cubed
4 potatoes, cubed
2 packages Lipton Onion Soup
2 cans cream of mushroom soup
1 1/2 cans of water
1 tsp. salt
1/2 tsp. pepper

Brown the stew meat. Add the rest of the ingredients. Bake in a heavy covered pan in a slow oven, 225 degrees, for 5-6 hours.

(Ann's note: She likes to add bay leaf, maybe some onion and a shot of red cooking wine.)

\* \* \* \* \*

As hard as college athletes sometimes try to project themselves as world-wise and sophisticated, usually they get exposed for what they are—kids.

The Cougars were on a trip to El Paso, having attended the Holiday Bowl the previous year. As the team bus made its way to the stadium that night, someone mentioned that from the freeway a person could see Mexico.

One young player remarked, "Geez, I didn't know El Paso and San Diego were that close together."

* * * * *

Trouble sometimes comes in the most innocuous way.

Gym Kimball was among a large group of gifted quarterbacks in the BYU program at the same time as Steve Young. Kimball was a noted free spirit. Caught in the logjam, Kimball eventually transferred to Utah State.

When he was still at BYU, he was talking with a teammate who suggested he greet defensive lineman Junior Filiaga, a Polynesian, with a traditional island greeting. Filiaga was reserved and soft-spoken.

"Say it to him," said the player, giving Kimball the word.

Kimball asked what it meant.

"It's a Polynesian greeting," he was told.

In the shower room, Kimball called out, "Hey, Junior!" and repeated the greeting.

Filiaga ignored him.

Hoping to impress his teammate with his command of the language, Kimball persisted.

"Junior!" he said. Then he repeated what he thought was a friendly island howdy-do.

That time Filiaga responded. He punched Kimball in the nose, then grabbed him by the neck and began banging his head against the wall tiles. Kimball later told teammates that every time his head hit the wall, his field of vision got smaller.

After washing the blood off his nose, Kimball began walking over to Filiaga to peacefully discuss the attack. Thinking Kimball might be seeking revenge, Filiaga began chasing him around the locker room.

"It was like he was putting on a pass rush," said Kimball.

It wasn't until later that he learned he had been set up. The word was a Polynesian vulgarity.

Sometimes just saying "Hi" is quite enough.

* * * * *

Ah, football, the game of precision. Eleven me
in unison, like the proverbial well-oiled machine—ea
component in the great scheme.

Or not.

By November 1, 1980, the Cougars had rolled to six straight
wins after a shocking opening-night loss to New Mexico. As they
moved along, they had become more imposing by the week,
scoring 41 points against Long Beach, 52 against Wyoming and
70 against Utah State.

All that was merely a precursor to the first game of November,
though.

Late in the game, with BYU leading Texas-El Paso 83-7—the
same day Edwards's daughter had her baby—the coaching staff
sent reserve quarterback Ryan Tibbitts in with the kickoff unit.
After getting in on the tackle, Tibbitts headed to the sidelines,
where he was intercepted by defensive backfield coach Dick Felt.

"Stay in at corner!" Felt yelled at Tibbitts.

"Take the right corner!"

*Huh?*

"I haven't played cornerback since high school!" Tibbitts
called back.

There was no turning back. Felt had decided to leave Tibbitts
in.

In hindsight, Tibbitts said he wasn't sure what prompted the
decision, but thought it could have been to send a message to
the second- and third-string cornerbacks, who hadn't been doing
the job the coaches wanted. So Felt called on someone from the
special teams.

Felt knew what he was doing. It's just that nobody else knew.

When he reached the huddle, linebacker Kyle Whittingham,
a team captain, took one look at the seldom-used Tibbitts and
said, "Tibbitts, get the hell out of here!"

"Coach Felt told me to come in," said Tibbitts.

"Why?"

"I don't know," said Tibbitts.

When they broke for the play, strong safety Kevin Walker
began calling out defensive signals. Trouble was, Tibbitts didn't

know the scheme.

"Shut up!" Tibbitts called back. "I don't know what you're talking about!"

He ended up playing two series, clueless as to what the defense was doing. Amazingly, nobody got loose for a touchdown.

After the game Whittingham stopped Tibbitts and apologized for trying to oust him from the huddle. "Sorry, man," said Whittingham. "I thought you got kicked in the head on that kickoff and didn't know where you were!"

\* \* \* \* \*

A good rule of thumb in college football is to stick close to the coach and the plane will never leave you behind.

At least that was the slogan of former sports information director Dave Schulthess.

In 1977, the Cougars played Oregon State in Corvallis. Afterward, the team boarded a bus and departed for Portland, where it was to catch the flight home.

Schulthess remained behind in the OSU athletic offices, where the Utah writers were sequestered, compiling their stories. One writer was particularly slow.

Schulthess, who was shuttling the writers to the airport, waited as long as he thought prudent, then began telling them they had only a few minutes remaining. That deadline passed. He told them again. Still, the one writer labored on.

Finally Schulthess said, "If you're not done in five minutes you'll have to find your own way home."

The writer finished his story and the group headed to the rental car. Schulthess was worried the team, which had absorbed a 24-19 loss to the Beavers, would be sweating and hungry on the plane—and angry about waiting for a bunch of reporters.

Schulthess and the group leaped in the car and tore off. As he whirled the vehicle around the corner, he looked to the sidewalk. There stood Coach Edwards with a Big Gulp in hand.

"I thought to myself, 'I love him,'" recalled Shulthess.

They never did discuss what had happened. Apparently

Edwards had been on the postgame radio show and assumed he would get a ride with Schulthess. Tired of waiting, he had walked to a nearby 7-Eleven for a drink—unbeknownst to anyone.

"Am I glad to see you," Schulthess said.

Now the pressure was off. The plane wasn't leaving without the coach.

About 30 miles farther, they were passing through a town when they saw a burger stand. Edwards said, "Let's get a malt."

Schulthess was astounded.

"I'd sooner have cut my throat than to stop for a malt, if it had been just me and the writers," said Schulthess.

Fortunately, they had The Man with them.

They stopped, got the malts and continued on without a care in the world.

When they arrived at the airport, they learned Schulthess had been right. The plane was full. The players were tired, hungry and waiting.

First one on the plane was Edwards.

Nobody said a word.

\* \* \* \* \*

There is one guarantee almost as safe as having the coach in your car: Having the school president.

Jim McMahon led the Cougars to a 28-3 rout of Wisconsin at Madison in 1980. Afterward, it was a similar scenario to the one in Corvallis, with the media working on stories and Schulthess waiting in the wings. Only this time, then-president Jeffrey R. Holland was with the traveling party.

Following the game, the team went to the airport. When the writers finished, and everyone got in the car, Schulthess reached in his pocket for the keys.

Nightmare on Elm Street.

The keys were gone.

He searched under the seats and around the car. Nothing doing. Thoughts raced through his mind. Was there time to take a taxi?

It was long after the game's end and the stadium was empty. Wracking his brain, Schulthess decided he might have left the keys in the press box. Inside the stadium, up the elevator, he was surprised to see the building was still open.

"The room was empty," recalled Schulthess. "I looked one way. Nothing. I looked the other way. Nothing. Then I noticed a slight glimmer as the sun was going down. I was saying, 'Please, please be the keys.' I walked toward it, and it was!"

Now there was just one more worry. They were so far behind the team, he was wondering how he would get the luggage transferred to the plane. They hopped in the car and drove off.

But even then, he wasn't too worried. After all, he had the university president with him. A couple of trips around the state capitol—he missed his turn at least twice—didn't faze him.

Through it all, he didn't get a single cross remark from President Holland.

And nobody complained when they got on the plane that time, either.

* * * * *

That game in Wisconsin was a BYU victory, thanks in large part Jim McMahon's attitude and talent.

And no thanks to the inadvertent signal-jamming that went on.

With part of the coaching staff in the press box to view the game, each was wearing a headset. But as the game progressed, they started getting strange signals.

"We're going to take delivery at 1142 Warren," said a voice in the headset.

Moments later: "We're gonna need another 25 or so in the southwest quadrant."

Occasionally, the coaches could hear someone saying, "It sounds like we're picking up a football game. What's going on?"

In the course of the action, delivery drivers for a local newspaper had found themselves on the same frequency as the headsets the BYU coaches were wearing. So in the end, it turned out a good deal for both parties. Besides winning the game, the Cougar coaches learned all about delivering newspapers. And the truck drivers learned some new routes.

\* \* \* \* \*

Most of college football is drama, excitement and even humor. But occasionally, there are moments of true sadness—and not just the passing type that comes with defeat.

In 1971, the Cougars were having a record-setting night. Golden Richards, whose style and talent matched his name perfectly, was enjoying a phenomenal game returning kicks.

At halftime, *Salt Lake Tribune* writer Bill Coltrin told Schulthess he was going to file his first-half summary, which he did. But as he sat down to settle in for the second half, he slumped over, then slid to the floor. He was dead of a heart attack.

Schulthess suddenly found himself in a crisis situation. Medical people were dispatched immediately to the press box. The game was unfolding and Schulthess had to phone the *Tribune* to inform editors that their writer wouldn't be filing the rest of the story.

Meanwhile, Hack Miller, a writer for the rival *Deseret News*, phoned the *Tribune* on behalf of Coltrin and dictated a story. It may have been the only time in history that a writer from one of the Salt Lake dailies filed for a rival.

\* \* \* \* \*

Prior to Edwards, there was at least one coach at BYU who wasn't a member of the Church of Jesus Christ of Latter-day Saints. That was Hal Kopp, who resided in Provo from 1956-1958, compiling a 13-14-3 record. That wasn't great, but it was a lot better than his predecessor, Chick Atkinson, who in seven seasons went 18-49-3.

Kopp was a lighthearted, jovial sort. Unfortunately for him, the administration wasn't quite as lighthearted and jovial.

After arriving at BYU, Kopp determined the Cougars needed

to pass more often. So he installed an offense that made more use of the air. According to Schulthess, on the train coming home from a road game, someone in the traveling party asked Kopp what made him decide to pass the ball that season.

"I put my head back and had a vision," said Kopp.

He went on to explain that he "saw an old pioneer, who had a long beard, and he was saying, 'Pass...pass...pass!'"

In Kopp's book, *I've Seen It All,* he wrote of sitting on a train with an assistant coach. The lights dimmed on the train, but another light appeared in the darkness. Three men were in the light. Kopp's account spoke of Brigham Young, Joseph Smith and another man he didn't know, appearing to him in a vision.

He went on to say Smith said, "You are in trouble, Coach," and spread his arms, indicating a spread formation. Then he made a passing motion. When Kopp said, "Pass the ball?" Smith nodded.

The "revelation offense" was born.

There is more than one inconsistency with Kopp's account, however. First, he wrote that his revelation came on the way home from a game "against the University of Montana at Bozeman." The University of Montana is in Missoula.

BYU never played Montana State, located at Bozeman, during his tenure.

Also, he said BYU lost 12-0. In his three seasons at BYU, the Cougars played Montana three times. They lost 21-14 in Missoula (1956), won 20-7 in Provo (1957) and won 41-12 in Missoula (1958).

That story about the revelation? Take it with a grain of salt.

Eventually Kopp left BYU and, at least in Schulthess's estimation, his departure may have been partially due to his sense of humor—which sometimes didn't go over with some of the more sober-minded folk in Provo.

"His irreverence may have proved to be his downfall," said Schulthess.

* * * * *

Kopp wasn't above playing a practical joke, either.

During those years in the late 1950s, the BYU Cougar Quarterback Club would meet at the Hotel Utah on a weekly basis. Kopp was required to be at the luncheons.

But he delighted in seeing the organizers sweat over whether he would be there on time.

One week, he came in plenty of time to make the luncheon, but looking around and seeing no one, sneaked behind the stairs and hid. Gradually the BYU boosters arrived. Eventually the organizers started wondering where Kopp had been sidetracked.

After a few minutes of waiting and wondering, the group suddenly saw Kopp, who walked in the door fashionably late.

"Maybe he figured if he was coming off a loss, that maybe it wouldn't be bad to see the fans sweat a little bit, too," Schulthess said.

\* \* \* \* \*

It would be hard to overstate the excitement in Provo in September of 1990. Coming off a conference championship and picked to win another, the Cougars had opened the season with a 30-10 win over UTEP.

Next up were the Miami Hurricanes, ranked No. 1 and defending national champions. In fact, the Hurricanes had won three of the previous seven national championships.

And BYU had them in Provo.

Prior to kickoff, the Cougars gathered in the locker room, first listening to the coach, then firing one another up. They stood in the tunnel, about to take the field, as a sold-out stadium began to roar.

George Curtis, the team trainer, was ready to go, too—which turned out to be a good thing. He had work piling up before the opening kickoff.

As the team stood in the tunnel, Rich Kaufusi, one of the BYU's players, tapped Curtis on the shoulder. "George," he said. "I need your help."

Strange. He had completed all the taping and wrapping. Why was he needed as they charged onto the field?

Curtis turned around to face a Cougar backup tight end, whose forehead was bleeding down his face and onto the front of his uniform.

"What happened to you?" Curtis said.

The player had been helmet-butting with Kaufusi in the locker room, getting excited for kickoff, when his chin strap slipped. His helmet slid up as he leaned forward to head-butt. Next thing he knew, Kaufusi's helmet had caught him in the forehead.

Blood everywhere.

"We haven't kicked off yet," recalled Curtis, "and already I have someone to patch up."

Curtis put some ice in a towel and taped it to his head.

"See you at halftime," said Curtis.

At the break Curtis and his staff had plenty to handle. Not only did the backup player receive 22 stitches, but quarterback Ty Detmer needed 11 on his chin.

Meanwhile, the coaches were mystified. When they came in, they saw the tight end with his head still bleeding. Wow. Tough game. Guys getting hurt without even being in the game.

\* \* \* \* \*

Curtis was always willing to play a practical joke, especially if it involved team members. He pulled one of them on highly regarded defensive lineman Shawn Knight.

In his first year at BYU, the six-foot-six, 280-pound Knight took a sports medicine class from Curtis. During one of the early sessions, Curtis said to the class, "I'd like to tell you how BYU ended up recruiting Shawn. Is that OK, Shawn?"

Unsure of where Curtis was going, Knight agreed.

Curtis continued: "You didn't play football until your senior year in high school, right?"

Knight nodded.

"And you played tennis and wrestled, too, right?"

Same reaction.

Curtis then told a fabricated story about Knight showing up at the office of LaVell Edwards, asking to play football. Edwards asked the young man how tall he was. He was told six foot eight. He asked Knight's weight: 280.

Curtis continued the tall tale thusly: "Son," Edwards said to Knight, "you're tall enough and you look big enough, but are you strong enough?"

Knight had a bearskin in tow and said he had killed a bear with his hands.

"OK," said Edwards, "you're strong enough. But are you fast enough?"

Knight held up a deerskin.

"OK. Looks like you're fast enough," Edwards continued. "But, son, can you pass a football?"

"Coach," Knight supposedly said, "I don't know. I've never swallowed one."

\* \* \* \* \*

In football, lots of people are tough. Yet one of the toughest guys ever to play at BYU is one few would suspect. It wasn't a linebacker, defensive lineman or tight end. Nor was it a running back.

It was a wide receiver.

Chuck Cutler played for BYU 1986-88. An All-Conference player his senior year, he was fearless in the face of oncoming cornerbacks.

One game, Cutler dropped a pass that seemed catchable. That was highly unusual for the sure-handed player. Earlier in the game he had bobbled a couple passes—also an oddity.

Finally, assistant coach Norm Chow approached Curtis and said, "What's wrong with Chuck? Find out what's wrong."

Curtis came to Cutler while the defense was on the field and asked about the problem.

"I'm fine," Cutler said.

"Coach Chow says you never drop passes," said Curtis.

Cutler reluctantly asked Curtis to look at his right hand. Sure enough, he had a broken thumb. Curtis asked to look at the other hand. That thumb was broken, too.

Cutler had just figured he could tell the training staff after the game.

He played with his fingers in splints the rest of the year.

\* \* \* \* \*

That wasn't Cutler's only difficult situation. The Cougars played at Air Force in November, working on what was for BYU a subpar 9-4 season. During the game, Cutler dropped to his knees to catch a low pass. A Falcon defender came in hard and flat to make the tackle, spearing Cutler in the back.

Cutler was slow getting up but didn't say a word. But between plays, Curtis noticed the wide receiver would sit rigidly on the bench.

"You OK?" said Curtis.

"Yup," was the reply. "Just resting."

The following day Cutler was in pain and asked Curtis for a treatment on his sore back. Curtis ordered an X-ray. To his surprise, he discovered the receiver had played most of the game with three broken transverse processes.

"He was one of the toughest guys we've ever had," says Curtis. "He never complained."

\* \* \* \* \*

It's a good thing the equipment people don't decide who plays.

When Cutler was a freshman, one of the coaches had him to go to the equipment room and ask for a pair of cleats. Cutler walked up to the window and made his request. The equipment person that day, Mel Darrington, handed Cutler a pair of old, worn shoes, a size or two too small.

"Here," he said. "Wear these. You'll never play anyway."

\* \* \* \* \*

Tight end Dave Mills (1981, 83-84) was another tough guy.

Former quarterback Robbie Bosco recalled playing at Wyoming one year with Mills. As the offense broke its huddle, he noticed Mills was heading the wrong direction. Something strange was up.

"Dave," said Bosco. "Where you going?"

"I can't see!" said Mills.

Bosco looked closer and noted Mills had a large cut above his nose, where his helmet had connected.

"Blood all over his face," recalls Bosco.

Mills never considered coming out of the game and Bosco never considered asking.

"You can't leave," said Bosco. "This is a big play. Come here."

When Mills got closer, Bosco took his quarterback towel and wiped his face off. Good enough.

Shortly after, he passed to Mills and the Cougars began a march that ended in a score.

\* \* \* \* \*

Similar story with offensive lineman Craig Garrick. There was something in his eyes, too. But it wasn't blood.

It was 1984, the year the Cougars won the national championship. When things got rolling, nobody wanted to miss a down. Especially Garrick.

After Bosco called a play in the huddle, he looked to see Garrick shaking his head. "I can't see!" he said.

Bosco could see dirt and grass all over Garrick's face. He had been smashed into the ground on a previous play and now his vision was blocked by dirt.

"Come here," said Bosco. When Garrick got close enough, Bosco took a deep breath and blew as hard as he could in his face. Dirt flew everywhere.

"All right! I can see now!" said Garrick.

Recalls Bosco, "That's how that season went. Guys always found ways to stay in the game. Nobody ever wanted to leave."

\* \* \* \* \*

Sometimes Cutler's toughness got the best of him.

For instance, the time he nearly ruined his engagement.

Cutler became engaged on a Thursday, during his junior year. The following Saturday, he was hit hard during the game and received a concussion. After the game Cutler was so affected, he was told to shower and dress, after which they would help him get to the hospital for observation.

They left him momentarily to attend to other duties, and when they came back, he was standing in the shower, fully clothed.

He was transported to the hospital for observation.

His fiancée showed up to check on his condition.

Said Cutler: "Who are you?"

Needless to say, he did some fast-talking the moment his memory returned.

\* \* \* \* \*

Other tough players came through the system such as offensive lineman Lloyd Fairbanks.

The 1974 Cougars were on their way to their first-ever bowl game, against Oklahoma State in the Fiesta Bowl. To Fairbanks' dismay, a week or so before the big game, he was stricken with appendicitis.

There went his postseason dreams.

But after the surgery, he kept insisting he could play in the game, even though a scant few days had passed.

"The morning of the game," recalled former defensive coach Tom Ramage, "he comes up to the team doctor and says, 'Doc, I want to play.' Doctor says, 'You can't play. You can't even get in a stance.'"

"I can play," repeated Fairbanks.

"Tell you what," said the doctor. "If you can get in the stance, and we can tape you up, you can play."

Next thing anyone knew, Fairbanks was down in a three-point stance.

Raring to go, a week after having his appendix removed.

"He won't make it through warmups," the doctor confided to Ramage.

Fairbanks not only started, but played the entire game.

\* \* \* \* \*

Concussions are a way of life in football. Still, they can get annoying—especially for those who don't have the concussion.

At the 1996 Cotton Bowl, receiver Kaipo McGuire was injured. In the course of the game, he was running a slant pattern across the field when he was taken out by a vicious hit. The impact knocked him out and gave him a concussion.

When he came to, he was lying on the field with the training staff surrounding him.

"George," he said to Curtis. "What up?"

Curtis told him he had sustained a concussion.

"Did I catch the ball?" he said.

Curtis told him it had been jarred loose.

"Bull crap," said McGuire. "I always catch the ball."

Seconds later, the same conversation was repeated with an assistant trainer.

Ned Stearns, a freshman, came across the field and asked Curtis if he could help.

"Yeah," said Curtis, as they helped McGuire off the field. "Stay with Kaipo and watch him. Don't let him go anywhere."

McGuire still wanted to ask anyone and everyone within earshot if he caught the ball. He repeated the same conversation with Stearns several times.

"Just tell him he caught it," Curtis said finally.

After the game, the teams vacated the field. When the Cougars got to the locker room, Curtis noticed McGuire was nowhere to be found.

Just then a Kansas State trainer walked in, leading the missing player.

"This guy yours?" he said.

McGuire had become so disoriented, he had gone into the K-State locker room.

* * * * *

Even with a concussion, some players know what to say. Or at least come close.

Linebacker Justin Ena sustained a concussion during a game in 1998. When the training staff got him to the sidelines, someone pulled off his helmet.

"I gotta play," Ena said. "I gotta play."

"Nope. You're finished for the day," said Curtis.

One key question trainers usually ask a player to determine if he has a concussion is simple: Who's your roommate?

When Curtis first told Ena he was out for the game, he said, "I know who my roommate is."

"Really," said Curtis. "Who?"

"Um…" said Ena.

Then he hugged Curtis.

"I gotta play," he repeated.

"Who's your roommate?" Curtis said again.

Ena didn't know.

So he wasn't going to play, after all.

But it was a nice try.

* * * * *

Curtis didn't remember all the players involved, but he remembered the play.

He told of the Cougars being at Arizona State one year, when an injury occurred. Then another. A string of injuries isn't unusual—unless it's to the same player.

This one happened while a player was being helped off the field.

Curtis had a rule that whenever a player was assisted to the sidelines, he needed to be helped by two teammates of approximately the same size as the injured party.

"In other words," Curtis said, "if I've got a 300-pounder hurt, I don't want two 180-pound backs taking him out of the game."

In the 1995 Arizona State game, BYU's Stan Raas, who weighed around 260 pounds, got hurt. But instead of similar sized players assisting, a pair of six-foot-three, 300-pound tackles came out to help. They were, according to Curtis, "way too tall."

Still, their intentions were good. So they picked him up and began carrying him off with his arms on their shoulders.

"Suddenly, I hear 55,000 people gasp," Curtis later recalled. He turned around to see Raas, planted in the stadium turf, face-first.

What had happened?

Because the two tackles were so tall that Rass couldn't touch the ground with his feet, he had put his arms on their shoulders and dangled his legs. As they walked off the field, Raas's shoulder pads rested against the arteries on the sides of his neck, cutting off circulation. Raas lost consciousness and pitched onto the turf.

The damages: a bloody nose, fat lip and, of course, the sprained ankle that initiated the attention in the first place.

\* \* \* \* \*

When you're a college student, you're poor.

When you're a college athlete, you're often poorer.

College football players have their housing, food, tuition and books paid, but that doesn't mean they have a lot of money. Vai Sikahema, for instance, recalled he and a number of other players had no spending money. They didn't have side jobs, so just scraping together enough money for dates was a major undertaking.

Thank heaven for recruiting cash.

"I owe the first three dates I went on with my [future] wife to recruiting," said the former kick-return star.

It went like this: When new recruits visited campus, the coaching staff would give a certain amount of cash to various players to take recruits out to the movies and dinner. What the coaches didn't know is that often the players would use the money to also ask out a date. It was the only time they had enough cash to take their girlfriends to the movies.

The new recruit would be told a BYU player would pick him up and show him around campus. Dinner and a movie would follow. There was just one catch: He wasn't always told it might be a threesome.

Sikahema recalled picking up a recruit and having him sit by the passenger window, with Sikahema's girlfriend in the middle.

"I wasn't the only one," he said. "We'd get together at a place called the Press Box, and there were always three or four guys there with dates—and a recruit. We didn't have a dime, normally."

In hindsight, it may not have been a terribly good recruiting tool, says Sikahema. "We probably weren't doing the school any favors. The recruit would have to sit the entire evening twiddling his thumbs while we were with our date."

Sikahema said he remembers hearing of highly recruited quarterback Sean Salisbury visiting BYU and ending up in a threesome.

"We always say that had as much to do with him going to USC as anything else. It just so happened that his 'host' had a coed on his arm."

\* \* \* \* \*

It's not often that someone in the press box can be credited with winning or losing a game. But it happens.

At least it did the time Arizona State got its inspiration from BYU's public address announcer.

In 1972, Arizona State was a dominant team in the conference. The Sun Devils had come to Cougar Stadium to play BYU in a late October game.

"It was a bad day," recalled Ramage. "It was snowing and cold. As we watched them warm up, we noticed they didn't have any cold weather gear."

When the Cougars went into the locker room, BYU public address announcer Kenner Kartchner went out of his way to welcome the Sun Devils to Provo. Over the speaker system he called it "the fastest team in America" and lavishly praised its talent.

As it turned out, the Sun Devils were as good as advertised, winning 49-17.

After the game, ASU coach Frank Kush had a conversation with Edwards. Said Ramage, "He told LaVell, 'You know, we were in big trouble. The kids were so cold they didn't want to play until the announcer started saying how great they were. Boy did that light a fire under them. Whoever your announcer is, I want to send him a letter of thanks!'"

* * * * *

One thing BYU players always appreciated about Edwards— he wasn't a drill sergeant. Whenever the team earned a bowl bid, he made sure players had the time to see some of the sights in the area.

For example, there was the annual trip to an aircraft carrier when the Cougars played in the Holiday Bowl.

The Cougars played in the 1976 Tangerine Bowl in Orlando. True to his philosophy, Edwards allowed the players to spend part of one day touring Cypress Gardens.

The day the team made its tour, Edwards had a speaking engagement. Immediately following his talk, he drove over to the Gardens to join his team. As he pulled up, he looked across one of the lakes and saw someone parasailing behind a boat, 30 feet above the water.

"Boy," said Edwards, "I hope that's not one of our players." Now why would he think that?

Moments later, the daredevil came down and glided toward the shore on water skis. "Stop!" said Edwards.

His fears had been realized. It was Cougar defensive tackle Mekeli Ieremia, cruising in for a landing.

And you wonder why coaches have trouble sleeping.

That incident didn't stop Edwards from granting his players free time during bowl weeks in the future. But it might have made him a bit more cautious.

\* \* \* \* \*

The worst plane trip ever for BYU? That's hard to say. Some of the long-ago adventures in the early days of flying have probably been lost over time.

The worst plane trip in recent history? Easy. The Washington game in 1997.

It was a perfect day for flying. Late summer, blue skies. The Cougars had chartered a flight to Seattle for the game against the Huskies.

Some of the staff and players felt only slightly nervous when they noticed as they boarded the plane in Provo that a mechanic in a tank top was pouring motor oil into the plane.

Oh well.

Because it was a smaller charter company, they didn't think much of it. But it was also a smaller plane. They were informed it would have to refuel in Boise.

Once the plane lifted off, all apprehensions were allayed— that is until they had been in the air about an hour. As they were flying over Mountain Home, Idaho, starting to descend into Boise, suddenly the plane took a near-nose dive, dropping some 500 feet. After the plane leveled out, the pilot got on the speaker system and informed the team that an alarm in the cockpit had ordered the plane to make a rapid descent. A jet from a nearby Air Force base had come into the general vicinity of the team charter, tripping the alarm that ordered the pilot to make the descent.

It was a routine procedural move.

When the plane landed in Boise to refuel, all was well, except one thing: A number of players refused to get back on the plane. Some wanted to take a bus or rent a car.

Eventually they all boarded and the rest of the trip was uneventful.

"It took quite a bit of time to convince a lot of our guys to stay on the plane," said director of football operations Duane Busby.

\* \* \* \* \*

One who certainly didn't appreciate the thrill ride to Seattle was then-quarterbacks coach Robbie Bosco.

The man never did like planes.

Some people don't like broccoli. Some don't like being in the water. Bosco, now BYU's Varsity Club director, makes it no secret he doesn't like flying. So much so, that he has been known to take sleeping pills to get through flights.

In the late 1990s, the Cougars were playing at New Mexico. A terrific storm came across the high desert, driving most of the fans out of the stadium. The game was even delayed briefly during the storm. Only a handful of spectators remained to see the outcome.

In the locker room after the game, Bosco was already planning ahead, asking a team doctor for a sleeping pill to help him get through the flight.

"It's pouring rain, lightning, thunder," said Bosco, years later. "As we're heading for the team bus after the game, I'm saying no way. I need to be out, now."

The doctor obliged. But by the time the team bus got to the airport, Bosco was still wide awake—and dreading the flight. So he asked for, and received, another sleeping pill.

As the bus rolled toward the airport, Bosco told Brian Mitchell, the cornerbacks coach, his garage code. Just in case he had trouble waking up.

He did.

Bosco slept the entire flight home. Back in Utah, coaches and staff couldn't wake him. They tried talking to him, shaking him. Nothing worked.

He was zonked.

"I remember them helping me off the plane, barely walking. I could hardly see in front of me. I'm out," said Bosco.

Mitchell carried him into his house and put him in bed. He didn't awaken until the following day—with a hazy memory of what happened and no memory of the flight home.

"Funny thing is," recalled Bosco, "they told me it was one of the smoothest flights home they had ever had."

\* \* \* \* \*

Because he was bashful and modest, this player's name will remain unexposed.

Too bad the same can't be said about his bare backside.

The Cougars were playing in a game at Utah, and one of Ramage's defensive linemen went wide to stop a sweep. The game was played on the old Ute AstroTurf, which was tough on knees, and even tougher on uniforms.

The Cougar lineman got knocked down on a play, and as he fell, he burned a large hole in the seat of his football pants.

Nevertheless, he executed one more play, as Ramage puts it, "with his fanny sticking out."

Following the play, he jogged to the sidelines. Ramage stuffed a towel in the player's pants and sent him back onto the field. When the teams changed possession, he went to the locker room and retrieved a new pair of pants.

It so happened that the player's fiancée and future mother-in-law were in the stands to see the whole episode.

According to Ramage, she said to her daughter, "Well, I think you picked a good boy. At least he's bashful."

\* \* \* \* \*

There are a lot of gentlemen at BYU.

It's just that there are more of them when the situation involves a woman and a missing bikini top.

BYU was playing in the Aloha Bowl in 1992. During the preparation week, a group of officials, coaches and players from the school took a field trip to look at the Blow Hole, a rocky outcropping with a hollowed-out area. When the tide comes in, the water shoots high into the air through the hole in the rocks.

That year, players were enjoying one of nature's wonders when their attention suddenly turned to another—a woman with her top off. She had been swimming in the area and when the tide came in, it swept off part of her bikini. She was stuck in the water and began calling for help.

It was her lucky day.

Or maybe theirs.

Five players jumped in to help out.

And they say chivalry is dead.

\* \* \* \* \*

Late in 1974, the Cougars' hopes were high. After dropping their first three games of the season—not such an unexpected occurrence in those days—they tied Colorado State in their fourth game. But after that, they went undefeated to earn their first bowl invitation. That year the Cougars represented the WAC in the Fiesta Bowl.

In the season's seventh game, BYU's players were starting to smell what looked like a historic season. They felt they were good, and by then their record was starting to improve quickly.

The game was at Arizona, a power in the old WAC. "We knew we had to beat Arizona, because if we did, we would be in pretty good shape to win the conference and go to our first bowl game," recalled Ramage.

The Wildcats had a running back that was one of the early players to celebrate after a touchdown. Back then it was new. To some, it was entertaining, to others merely galling.

For Ramage, the end zone celebrating fell into the latter category.

After watching game films of the Arizona player's antics, several of Ramage's defensive soldiers began talking about sacking the player and dancing over him. But when Ramage overheard the conversations, he intervened.

"I said, 'No. I'll make you a better deal. What we've got to do is beat them, on national TV, and as soon as we do, you can get together and dance on the field. That would really pour salt in the wound.'"

Only problem was beating Arizona.

But the game day came, and the Cougars had an exceptional outing, beating the Wildcats 37-13. At game's end, Ramage looked onto the field. There were all his "big guys" dancing in the middle of the field, in the rain.

*Vai Sikahema (right) made the most of his
opportunity when called upon to help with recruiting.
(Photo by Mark Philbrick, BYU Photo)*

"No one," said Ramage, "knew what they were doing. They were just out there doing this dance. All those great big guys, trying to do a little jig. People were asking, 'What in the world is this?' But we knew."

He who dances last, dances best.

\* \* \* \* \*

Recruiting can be mean. It can be nasty. And sometimes it can be downright unethical.

Chuck Ehin was a highly recruited defensive tackle from Utah. Coming from high school, numerous big-name colleges recruited him.

After considerable soul searching, Ehin narrowed his choices to BYU and Alabama. At that time, in the late 1970s, Bear Bryant was still prowling the sidelines for the Crimson Tide.

The day before the signing date, Ehin got a telegram from Alabama. The note apologized for the bad news, but said Bryant had waited too long for Ehin to make up his mind. Thus, the Alabama football program could no longer honor its scholarship offer. The school was moving on.

Signed, Bear Bryant.

The next day, when BYU's Edwards showed up at Ehin's home to sign him to a letter of commitment, he asked what had happened to Alabama. Ehin told Edwards of the telegram.

"What telegram?" said Edwards.

When Edwards was shown the letter, he noted it was signed "Bear" Bryant.

Having been involved with Bryant numerous times over the years, Edwards knew something Ehin didn't—Bear Bryant never signed his letters "Bear." He always signed it by his real name, Paul.

Edwards immediately made a call to Bryant, telling him he knew something was wrong and that if Ehin wanted to go to Alabama, he would be willing to agree. But Ehin declined, saying the whole incident must have had a reason. He signed with BYU anyway.

In the years since, suspicion has persisted about the origin of the bogus Alabama rejection letter. One theory is that it came from a Colorado assistant coach. The reasons for that are unclear. A more logical theory is the mysterious telegram came compliments of an Auburn booster, who didn't want to see Ehin playing for Alabama.

Who knows?

As they said in *The X-Files,* the truth is out there.

\* \* \* \* \*

The late Rex Lee was not only a popular president at BYU, but an unabashed Cougar sports fan. He was often seen on trips with the football team. It was a job he was more than happy to perform.

Lee enjoyed teasing colleagues that he knew a great deal about football. One of his favorite tricks was pretending he could tell what play the Cougars would run. Just before kickoff at Cougar Stadium, Lee would approach offensive coordinator Norm Chow and ask what the first play of the game would be. Chow might say the Cougars would open with a screen, an off-tackle slant or even a surprise reverse. Whatever the plan, he would always tell Lee. (It never hurts to have the school president on your side.)

Lee would then retire to the president's booth, where he would be entertaining guests, often general authorities of the LDS Church. Just before the Cougars took over for their first possession, Lee would say, "You know, I've been watching this team a lot. And if I know anything about football, I have a hunch they're going to run an inside screen on the first play of the game."

Sure enough, the first play would be an inside screen.

Which served two purposes: It usually got the Cougars some yardage, and it always impressed the president's guests.

\* \* \* \* \*

Longtime linebackers coach Ken Schmidt was a popular and agreeable member of the staff. But that didn't mean he couldn't be provoked.

One of those occasions was at a football game in Logan.

In the late 1990s, the Cougars were at Romney Stadium for a game against Utah State. Included on the Cougar roster was Hans Olsen, nephew of Utah State legends Merlin and Phil Olsen.

This, of course, rankled many of the Aggie fans, who had never quite forgiven another Olsen, Orrin, for going to BYU. Now it was Hans who had defected to the south.

"We were playing Utah State, and of course, that's where my uncles had gone," said Hans Olsen, "and Utah State was really mad at me for not going to their school, but I followed in Orrin's footsteps and went to BYU."

As the game progressed, some of the Aggie fans began taunting the youngest Olsen for not playing at USU. "There are these drunken idiots in the stands, screaming at me, 'You traitor! How could you have done this to our school?'" continued Olsen.

"I look over into the stands and about 10 rows up was my grandma. She attends every Utah State game and she's just shaking her head because these guys around her are so belligerent.

"So I start walking over to these guys to tell them to shut up. They know it's my grandma and they're saying, 'Hans, your grandma doesn't want to talk to you, she's so ashamed you went to BYU!'

"So I got mad at those guys and I'm going to go after them, when Coach Schmidt comes over and grabs me and says, 'Hans, get back on the sidelines! Get back!' So I walk back and I look over and Schmidt grabs a water bottle and he just chucks it at those guys. Then he yells at them to shut up.

"He says, 'If you guys have a problem, I'll meet you after the game!'"

Concluded Olsen, "I couldn't believe it. I'm like, 'That's my boy, Coach!'"

\* \* \* \* \*

There are close calls and then there are close calls.

BYU's last-second win over SMU? Close. The Cotton Bowl win over Kansas State? A squeaker.

Almost apprehended for packing marijuana in your gym bag? Dangerously close.

Despite BYU's clean image, there have always been a few players who got around the honor code system. Such was the case of one Cougar player—who will remain unnamed—in the 1978 Yokahama Bowl.

That year, the Cougars had been sent to Japan to play in a postseason quasi-exhibition game. The idea was to introduce football to the Orient. The Cougars ended up beating UNLV 28-24.

Although all turned out well, it could have been a disaster. Ray Linford, an offensive lineman on that team, recalled traveling with his wife on the trip. (School officials allowed married team members to bring their spouses.)

As they were going through customs in Tokyo upon arrival, security personnel began rustling randomly through bags, looking for contraband. As they were searching the bags, one of the BYU players leaned close to Linford and whispered, "I sure hope they don't search my bags."

When Linford asked why, the player said he had marijuana stashed inside.

The officials ended up searching Linford's bags, but skipped the other player's—which was a fortunate thing for the player and a lucky thing for BYU. It could have been a public relations disaster.

Sometimes, the closest calls aren't on the field.

\* \* \* \* \*

There have been some great linebackers from BYU—some great tight ends, offensive linemen, receivers and running backs, too.

But make no mistake. Quarterback is still the glamour position.

Bosco learned that firsthand in 1984 during homecoming week.

The occasion was the traditional bonfire. Students and fans had gathered to rally for the upcoming game. Edwards assigned receiver Glen Kozlowski, lineman Craig Garrick and Bosco to attend the festivities in the parking lot west of the stadium. When they arrived, each was supposed to speak a few moments. First, team captain Garrick said a few words, but the crowd was fairly quiet.

"We gotta get this crowd pumped up," Koz whispered to Bosco. "Let me have the microphone!"

Kozlowski got the microphone, pointed to the "Y" on the mountainside, and screamed, "Every time I look up at that 'Y' lit up on the mountain, I get *fired up! Fired up!*"

Dead silence.

Nothing.

Kozlowski dropped the microphone and walked away.

Then it was Bosco's turn.

Bosco, it should be noted, wasn't a big talker in college. He was quiet and modest. But it *was* his turn.

He began mumbling a few words about winning the game, their undefeated record, *blah, blah, blah.*

The crowd went bonkers.

Why did the crowd love what he had to say?

Easy. He was the quarterback.

\* \* \* \* \*

In the early 1970s, airport security wasn't what it is today. But it wasn't totally relaxed, either.

Even then, you didn't want to mention a bomb.

On the way to Phoenix for the 1974 Fiesta Bowl, the Cougars were going through the Salt Lake Airport security gate. One of the players had a Christmas package that was wrapped and tied nicely. As they went through the checkpoint, a security agent asked what was in the box.

Another player wisecracked, "It's a bomb."

Before they knew it, the comedian/football player was being investigated by security. Coaches, administrators, equipment people and others ended up talking to airport officials to get their player on the plane.

"They had him out of there so fast it wasn't funny," said Ramage.

Which goes to show that joking about bombs at an airport was never funny. And it's a bad way to get to your destination on time.

\* \* \* \* \*

It's no surprise to know that for years Hawaii considered BYU its biggest rival. But it was difficult playing there for another reason: creeping, crawling and swimming things.

One year when BYU played in the Islands, the coaching staff let players out for a brief swim. But one player ended up getting zapped by a stingray. The coaches took him to a hospital and got him treated.

"He looked pretty sick," recalled Ramage.

Still, he was well by game time.

That same trip, one of the linebackers was preparing for the game. He stuck his hand in a protective glove and let out a yelp. Pulling off the glove, he noticed a centipede crawling out. He too was treated, and the incident never became serious.

"Those Hawaii people kept telling us we needed to shake our equipment out first," said Ramage. "After that, we did."

Thereafter, the Cougars visited the Islands with two warnings.

First, watch out for nasty linebackers.

And second, watch out for unusual creatures.

\* \* \* \* \*

Everyone knew about Dick Felt's infamous checklist. And everyone but Dick Felt worried about it.

Throughout his long career as a BYU assistant coach, Felt was famous for his ubiquitous sheet by which coaches kept track of players. As they would get on the team buses, Felt would check off the names.

Trouble was, Felt always used the same list for the entire trip. The first time the team went somewhere, he would check off each name, one by one. But when they got on the bus for another excursion, he would try something else. Sometimes it was a star, a line or a squiggle through the name. By the end of the trip, it was hard to decipher which players were on the bus and which weren't. The checklist was a mess.

The 1985 Cougars played in the Citrus Bowl. True to form, Felt had his checklist up and running. By the time game day arrived, the list looked like Egyptian hieroglyphics—a star here, sun there, maybe a serpent or an ox.

That year, the team boarded the buses and Edwards said, "Dick, everyone here?"

"Yeah," said Felt. The buses left for the stadium.

When they arrived, Ramage looked around and said, "Where's Jason Buck?"

Nobody had seen Buck.

"How about Shawn [Knight]?"

No answer.

Two other starters were missing, as well.

Somehow, Felt had confused his markings and thought the four players were on board.

Just before warmups, the missing players arrived, having caught a ride with someone attending the game. They were late but safe.

"Dick was famous for that list," said Ramage. "He would use the same sheet the whole trip. By the time it was over, you couldn't tell who was on the list."

* * * * *

Air Force was notorious for its grabbing and low cut-blocking. So much so, that sometimes teams over-prepared.

When Claude Bassett was a linebackers coach at BYU, he thought he had a plan. The idea was to fight fire with fire. He would have his players practice cut-blocking, the way Air Force blocked, and thus have his defensive players ready to go when the game began.

On the day of the game, Bassett brought his players out onto the field against a unit of surrogate offensive linemen, pretending to be Falcons. He had told them to go ahead and try blocking and grabbing defensive players by the ankle, to try to simulate the Air Force method.

The blockers did such an effective job, BYU already had

injuries before the game began.

"We get out there," said Ramage, "and Shad Hansen[middle linebacker, 1989-92] already had a sprained ankle. He could hardly walk. We had a couple of others hurt, too. And that was before the game even started. They didn't play too well, either."

As with movies and books, reality can be good.

Too much reality is dangerous.

\* \* \* \* \*

Mike Holmgren wasn't a member of the Church of Jesus Christ of Latter-day Saints. But he quickly learned a thing or two about coaching at a Mormon school when he worked there as an assistant coach.

One of the biggies: Watch your language—at least when someone's watching.

Holmgren could get fired up when he was trying to make a point. One day in the locker room, he was ranting about something or another, when he let slip with a well-known expletive.

"I'm sure LaVell had told him not to do that," said former return star Vai Sikahema (1980-85). "He was a young coach and so passionate, and one day he lets the word drop. It was like the old E. F. Hutton commercial—the entire room went quiet."

In the middle of his rant, Holmgren stopped "dead in his tracks and composed himself."

Twenty seconds of silence ensued. Then he resumed in a normal tone.

When E. F. Hutton talks, everyone listens. When a BYU coach talks, same thing…if he uses a certain word.

\* \* \* \* \*

One thing that really bugged the BYU defensive line in the late 1990s was the practice drill in which players were ordered to run through a rope ladder. It was a common drill, but that didn't make it more palatable.

Linemen Issiah Magalei and Hans Olsen were discussing what

a pain the rope drill was. It was 25 feet or so of anguish, especially if you weighed 300 pounds.

"It was the most tiring part of practice," said Olsen.

Somewhere along the way, several players came up with a great plan: cut off some of the rope. Defensive line coach Ramage would never know. So they did. After practice one day, one of the players sneaked out and severed several feet from the rope, hurling it over the fence surrounding the practice field. He left the rest of it alone.

The following day as they were running drills, Ramage looked perplexed. "I'll be danged if that rope doesn't look shorter," he said.

"Same way it always was to me," said one lineman.

"Looks the same to me," said another.

"I swear that rope looks shorter," Ramage insisted.

They went back and forth, debating whether the rope had been shortened, throughout the practice.

The following day, Olsen went on the other side of the fence to find the rope rungs. They were nowhere in the vicinity. After asking around, he discovered Magalei had taken them home and hung them on his apartment wall as a trophy.

In the next few days, word began to spread on the team that the linemen had severed the ropes. Fearful one of the coaches would visit his apartment, Magalei threw the rungs back behind the fence. There they lay until debris and leaves covered them.

About a month later, a large wind came up and blew away the leaves. By that time, Ramage knew he had been duped. He walked over to where the ropes had been hurled. There, amid the leaves, was the evidence.

Ramage, however, didn't attempt to reattach the rope.

Practices were never again as tough as they once were.

# CHAPTER 10

## *The Bronco Era*

BYU had been through the LaVell Edwards era, in which the famous coach's imperturbable sideline demeanor reigned. It had been through the uneven Gary Crowton period, when the program went from an exhilarating start to a demoralizing finish.

Then came the guy with the B-western movie name.

Bronco Mendenhall became just the third BYU coach in 33 years when he replaced Crowton in December 2004, having moved up from defensive coordinator.

He wasn't BYU's first choice. That was Kyle Whittingham, who agonized about whether or not to stay at Utah, where he had been a defensive coordinator himself. When Whittingham chose the Utes, BYU chose Mendenhall over respected assistant Lance Reynolds.

Mendenhall was a considerable departure from Crowton. While Crowton was impulsive in his play calling, and prone to unfiltered remarks (remember "I'd rather win by nine than two" after passing on first-down, deep in his own territory, late in a loss?), Mendenhall was guarded. The latter still tends to come off as mechanical, using words such as "manifest," "collective" and "invested."

But that's just his public image, according to NFL player and former BYU linebacker Bryan Kehl.

When Kehl was playing in Provo (2002, 2005-2007), the team would meet at 2:10 each afternoon before practice. One Halloween day, someone came up with the idea for every player to arrive at the meeting dressed like Mendenhall, which meant wearing a BYU hat and shorts, a knee band, and a play chart tucked into his pants.

It was the way Mendenhall dressed every day for practice. His norm was to stand outside the team auditorium and greet each player. This time the players filed in one at a time, curtly nodding back in Mendenhall manner and walking by in the Mendenhall uniform.

"One after one they filed in and—in the stoic Bronco Mendenhall way— gave him a nod. He was just standing there loving it," Kehl said, recalling the day.

After all had been seated, the coach momentarily stayed outside the room, then walked in. To the players' surprise, he had returned looking suspiciously like them. As Kehl put it, "With catlike quickness he walks in with his hat on backward and sideways [a la Austin Collie], shorts halfway down his seat, shirt un-tucked—he struts in imitating us."

Said Kehl: "It was hilarious. I almost wet my pants laughing. He did it so quick and countered back."

This side of Mendenhall never shows when the media is around.

"The public only gets the tip of the iceberg with Bronco," Kehl said. "He's fairly open with [LDS] firesides, but when the media's around, he is zipped shut. He doesn't let anything out. But with the players, it's a whole different thing. Bronco is a funny, funny guy."

\* \* \* \* \*

BYU—it's not for everyone.

Mendenhall's coaching methods? Same thing.

When Mendenhall arrived at BYU, running back Curtis Brown had just finished his junior season. The next fall the Cougar coach took his team onto the field at Edwards Stadium and had players lie on the grass. He had arranged for some of BYU's greatest victories to be broadcast over the loudspeakers.

It worked well enough, at least for the players who grew up

in Utah.

For the others, not so much.

"It's interesting because for a lot of guys, especially if you're LDS, you grow up around that tradition," Brown acknowledged several years later. "You watch it on TV."

Brown didn't. Thus when Mendenhall had the memory moments pumped through the loudspeaker system, Brown just looked around.

"I'll be honest. It's tough," Brown later said. "I bought into a lot of what Coach Mendenhall wanted to do. Some (players) didn't necessarily buy into it all the way, so you go through the motions."

For instance, there were the memento coins Mendenhall had his players carry around, with that year's slogan imprinted. Players were told to prepare to produce the coins on demand, as a symbol of unity.

There were also the infamous "Quest for Perfection" tee shirts in 2008 (BYU went 10-3 but lost conference games to Utah and TCU).

"[The coins] were a little corny and we kind of made fun of it, but we made the most out of it," former quarterback Max Hall said in retrospect.

Brown went on to note he wasn't a Utah native and thus hadn't memorized all of Jim McMahon's and Ty Detmer's exploits. "The deal is, I respect Coach Mendenhall. I supported him 110 percent. I knew some things he asked of us were not in my comfort zone, but I was willing to make an effort because I felt unless I bought into it 110 percent, I wouldn't succeed."

Wise move. In Brown's years at BYU, the Cougars went 5-7, 5-6 and 6-6 under Crowton but 11-2 under Mendenhall.

\* \* \* \* \*

"Fourth-and-18," Max Hall was saying in February of 2013, more than five years after the play. "One of my favorite plays of all time."

For him and a million others.

LaVell Edwards Stadium had fallen silent on November 24, 2007. The Cougars were on their own 12-yard line, trailing 10-9 in the Utah-BYU game with 1:13 to go.

A sack on first down had been followed by two incomplete pass attempts to Dennis Pitta. One try remained.

Hall told all his receivers to "go 90," which meant straight downfield, full speed—except Collie.

"For some reason I told Austin, 'Give me a stutter-go,'" said Hall.

A 12-yard route, a fake curl, then run for the border.

Hall dropped back, stepped inside the rush, rolled right and let it fly.

"When Austin stuttered, the cornerback thought I was going to run, so he came up two steps and let Austin get behind him," Hall said. "Unbelievable."

It wasn't exactly a rocket launch. Hall had been playing with ligament damage to his throwing shoulder.

"Austin was wide open," Hall said. "I cocked the ball back and threw it as high and as far as I possibly could. I think it only went 15 or 20 yards."

It turned into a 49-yard play. The Cougars still had 39 yards to the end zone, but the damage had been done. A couple of penalties on Utah plus a bruising run by Harvey Unga and the Cougars had a touchdown, leading to a 17-10 win.

"My heart was beating so hard—*boom! boom! boom!*—and the place just erupted. It was the loudest I ever heard it. I was vibrating," Hall continued.

After the game Collie remarked to reporters, "I wouldn't say it was lucky. We executed the play well… obviously, if you do what's right on and off the field, I think the Lord steps in and plays a part in it. Magic happens."

That quote was widely criticized by Utah fans, many of which felt the implication was that Heaven favors BYU. Hall said Collie was just pointing out that if players prepare well, live wisely and work hard, good things result.

That should go without saying, Hall observed in 2013. Then he paused as the memory of that day flooded back.

Quarterback Max Hall said the furor over his Utah comments surprised him. He added that people shouldn't take his I-hate-Utah rhetoric as seriously as they do. (AP photo/Douglas C. Pizac)

"So we won," he said with a slight laugh, pausing for a beat. "Fourth-and-18."

* * * * *

Former Baltimore Ravens linebacker Ray Lewis isn't the only football guy who cries.

John Beck was just a freshman in 2003 when called upon by then-coach Gary Crowton to quarterback the Cougars against Air Force, a 24-10 loss at LaVell Edwards Stadium. Afterward, in the press interview room, Beck made an offhand remark that would haunt him for several years. As cameras rolled and pens scratched he said, "I hate to lose, I hate it."

Blinking back tears, he added the immortal rejoinder: "This is probably going to ruin my weekend."

Not to mention his reputation.

But that was only temporary. Though BYU finished 4-8 that year, when Beck was a senior under Mendenhall, he led the Cougars to an 11-2 season and a Las Vegas Bowl win over Oregon.

Although the bowl win was satisfying, nothing was more memorable than his last-second misdirection pass to Harline on the final play of the 2006 game against Utah.

That time, nobody laughed at his tears...

* * * * *

It was all in the eyes.

The 2006 Utah-BYU game had gone as it always did. It was intense and personal. BYU had a timeout with only three seconds remaining, trailing 31-27 at Utah's Rice-Eccles Stadium. Robert Anae, the offensive coordinator, told his group, "We got one play."

When the snap came, John Beck momentarily looked left, then rolled right under pressure, keeping his eyes right as well. The clock ran out. He looked right, right, right.

And there was Jonny Harline.

Left.

Standing in the end zone, like a solitary man waiting for a bus.

"I knew my assignment," former running back Curtis Brown

would say years later, "but I had no idea what routes they were running. I just ran in the end zone and tried to make myself as small as possible. John had an arm and could throw into a small pocket if someone was there in a crouch. I squatted down and stayed there. I figured everybody else could just figure out what they were going to do."

It's not like there was much actual play execution at that point, anyway. Everything had broken down. One Utah player came close to grabbing Beck, another hit him immediately after he released the ball.

"It was a broken play and Jonny was going against the grain," Brown said. "Typically when the quarterback holds the ball that long [11 seconds], you go where the eyes are. John was running to the right side and his eyes were on the right side of the field. Little did they know Harline was going the opposite direction."

Beck lofted a long, cautious pass that Harline caught on his knees for the win.

Some who were there said it was bedlam, even though the game was at Utah's Rice-Eccles Stadium. Others said it was just plain weird.

"It was silent at first. I see John get tackled (after the pass) and then I hear cheering. I honestly thought we'd lost, our fans were cheering so loud," Harline said last February.

He continued, "I didn't think he'd seen me back there. I was behind everyone. He rolled and it was kind of natural for everybody to follow the quarterback. That's what you're taught as a receiver is to follow the quarterback. In that case, it looked pretty crowded over there, I thought, 'If I hang back here, if he see's me, I'll be wide open.'"

Harline said he didn't worry about dropping the pass as it sailed his way.

"People ask me if I was afraid. I wasn't nervous about it at all. I knew I'd catch it."

He also knew he'd get dog-piled.

"I caught the pass and jumped up and everyone tackled me," Harline said, "and John got lifted up on everyone's shoulders. So I got the bad end of that."

Harline's brother jumped the fence and ran onto the field after the PAT, with security people in hot pursuit. The brotherly reunion lasted, oh, three seconds.

"I didn't say much, then he was running off again," Harline said.

Curiously, Harline didn't say a word to the Utes. It had been "a mean, emotional game, a lot of trash-talking on both sides, not a lot of good feelings toward each other."

Yet after the PAT, Harline said he thought about taunting the Utes but refrained. Later he was momentarily angry with himself for not saying anything, though "looking back, I'm glad I didn't."

Sometimes there's nothing left to say.

*  *  *  *  *

Then there are those who are just fine with saying something.

Of all the controversies involving BYU and Utah, none stirred up the rivalry more than quarterback Max Hall's post-game comments after a 26-23 Cougar win in 2009.

He was sorry he said it. Or at least the way he said it.

But sorry he thought it?

Please.

It happened in the unlikeliest of places –the post-game interview room at LaVell Edwards Stadium. Media were asking the usual questions about the game, the rivalry, etc. Suddenly, Hall spoke up.

"I don't like Utah," he said. "In fact, I hate them."

Had he really said that?

Totally.

"I hate everything about them. I hate their program, I hate their fans—I hate everything. So it felt really good to send those guys home. They didn't deserve it. It was our time and it was our time to win. We deserved it. We played as hard as we could tonight and it felt really good, again, to send them home and get them out of here, so [it was] a game we'll always remember."

Asked to elaborate, Hall added, "I think the whole university, their fans, the organization's classless. I think, you know, they threw beer on my family and stuff last year, and did a bunch of nasty things, and I don't respect them and they deserve to lose."

Hall's remarks were either fantastic or, well, classless, depending on whom you ask. One thing seemed obvious: He had been thinking about it. But that's where the story gets mixed. Hall has since said that Utah fans abused his parents the previous year in Salt Lake, surrounding them after the game and pelting them with insults, debris and beer. Utah fans argue that beer is banned at the stadium and say Hall also claimed his relatives had beer poured on them by Arizona fans, back when he was at ASU.

In any case, Hall apologized the day after the Utah-BYU game.

"I want to take the opportunity to clarify and apologize for a few of my remarks after the game yesterday," he said in a statement released by the school. "Last year [at Rice-Eccles Stadium], my family was spit on, had beer dumped on them and were physically assaulted on several occasions. They had to endure extremely vile comments personally attacking my wife, my mother, other family members and our religion. They had to be escorted to their car by local police.

"As a result of what happened to my family last year, this rivalry became personal, and in the heat of the moment yesterday, I made comments toward the entire university that were really directed specifically at those fans in RES. It was not intended to be directed at the entire organization and all of their fans, and I apologize that it came out that way."

Hall generally didn't comment on the incident again for a few months afterward, saying the formal apology would suffice. But that didn't stop it from becoming a quote for the ages. To this day Utah fans can be seen with red tees or bumper stickers that say "Max Hall hates me."

Hall said he didn't originally think his comments would be that big a deal, but media coverage was gigantic. Still, he didn't get any backlash from Mendenhall or teammates. He nowadays contends they all agreed in spirit. After all, Utah is BYU's rival.

"Everybody (on the team) thought it was funny," Hall said in early 2013. "The people I feel bad for is the ones who take it seriously. It really upset a lot of people. I'm like, *come on!*"

\* \* \* \* \*

If Collie's "magic" remarks in 2007 were sensational, Hall's 2009 rant was flat-out epic.

In 2008, he had thrown five interceptions in a loss to Utah. But the next year he found Andrew George across the middle as two Utah players collided. Hall was hit on the play, but by then the ball was winging its way to history.

"I took a shot on the play but I remember looking up on my back and seeing two Utah guys on their backs and Andrew running downfield. That was awesome," Hall said.

Afterward, the old wounds resurfaced. Hall remembered his anger from the previous year. He remembered his family. He thought about the bumper stickers and taunts after his poor game the year before.

"For a full year, I had to listen to it, 'Max Hall's turnovers,' all kinds of stuff…people just making fun of me, which is fine. But it wears on you," he later said.

By the time he got to the next season, he had a lot stored up.

"I had been mad for a long time; for a year," he said, recalling his famous rant.

Hall even warned the public relations staff what was coming. As he walked from the locker room to the media interview room, he told BYU media relations staffers: "I apologize in advance."

"They were like, *no, no, no,* but I just went and said what I said," Hall recalled.

Three years later, he reiterated his remarks, saying, "The only thing I wish that I had not said was [the part about] the whole university. If I had just said the rest—I don't even really care that I said I hate Utah, because I hate them—if I'd said I hate Utah, and how their fans treated my family as being classless, instead of the whole university being classless—that's not what I meant. But what happened [to my family] was not right."

Then Hall said what he said, one more time.

"It felt really good to send those guys home and to beat them."

It's no secret: Max Hall still hates Utah.